The Church in Southeast Asia

The Church in Spain

THE CHURCH IN

Winburn T. Thomas & Rajah B. Manikam

SOUTHEAST ASIA

with an introduction by
FRANK T. CARTWRIGHT

FRIENDSHIP PRESS

New York

Library of Congress Catalog Card Number: 56-7954

Contents

Two CONVICTIONS undergird this study. The first is that the focus of our attention upon the younger churches should be the resultant Christian communities rather than the missionary relationships. We therefore have sought to treat the life and work of each of the Christian churches as indigenous units rather than as extensions of Western churches. Thus it was thought best that the study be written jointly by a Westerner and an Asian Christian leader. We do not profess to have developed this emphasis fully. We hope that we have made a beginning that will induce writers of coming study books to concentrate their attention upon the emerging Christian communities and the permeation of non-Christian cultures with Christian ethical idealism.

Secondly, we have approached our field ecumenically. Dr. Walter Horton in his *Christian Theology: An Ecumenical Approach* states that a sectarian theology is as absurd as a "Baptist astronomy." We are convinced that the story of the church's expansion must be treated as a whole rather than in terms of denominational extensions. While the men and the money that make the extension possible are denominational and national in character, their impact is primarily Christian. National and sectarian lines become blurred as they strike non-Christian cultures and secular philosophies. Christians of all varieties find themselves cooperating to an extent undreamed of in the lands where the differences developed. The extension of one variety of Christianity opens the way for other groups to follow—witness the flooding of Japan and Taiwan with sectarian missionaries since 1945 and the rapid growth of Protestantism in the Roman Catholic Philippines since 1898.

While Western missionary education and giving is organized along denominational lines, we believe that sending societies will increasingly enlarge the ecumenical projects item in their budgets to undergird Christian communities, movements, and institutions that are inadequately supported. Church World Service, Orphaned Missions, and the Asia Council of Ecumenical Mission are but a foretaste of the developments due to come in the world-wide extension of Christianity.

WINBURN T. THOMAS

I, RAJAH B. MANIKAM, joint author of this book, have had the unusual privilege of acting for the last five years as East Asia secretary of the World Council of Churches and the International Missionary Council. This was the first appointment of its kind in the history of Southeast Asia, and it has afforded me a wonderful opportunity to learn to know the churches in this area, to work with and for them, and to share their joys and sorrows. These young churches in these old lands of Southeast Asia are minority churches set amidst vast numbers of non-Christians, and they therefore face many problems.

But thank God they are there—in every one of these countries—and however small they may be, they are the hope of their countries. The older churches in North America are in partnership with them; therefore, the facts presented in this book, I hope, will kindle a living interest in them and evoke a response, both in personnel and finance. The churches in these ancient lands of Southeast Asia beckon to their partners in North America to come over and help them. May God help many to hear this Macedonian call! This time it comes from Southeast Asia.

RAJAH B. MANIKAM

INTRODUCTION

"INDONESIA is different" is a statement used often by an
American who has been called the best informed Westerner
in Indonesia. He speaks truly; Indonesia is different. But
Burma is also, and so are Malaya, Thailand, Indochina, and
the Republic of the Philippines. Each differs markedly from
the others, and Southeast Asia as a whole differs from the
other geographical areas I have visited. This is part of the
charm they possess for us who know them, but it serves to
introduce the baffling problems presented in this book.

Concerning the Christian movement in these lands of
Southeast Asia, the authors of *The Church in Southeast Asia*
have written informatively and with interpretive insight. In
all too brief compass, they have given many facts regarding
each country—its geographic outline, its population, its economic strength and weakness, and its culture. At greater
length, but still incompletely because of the space limits
imposed, they have dealt with the churches and the Church.
The book should prove to be a valuable aid in answering
here in the West the questions so often asked in local church
groups and in larger gatherings of Christians, questions such
as: "Just what is the 'challenge of Southeast Asia'?" "Why
should we Christians of North America send missionaries to
this area overseas?" "If, as we hear, the missionary era is at
an end in Asia, why should we give money for churches,
schools, and hospitals over there?" "For that matter, is there

any real need or desire for us to send missionaries to Asia?"

In his stimulating and provocative book, *Christian Missions and the Judgment of God,* David M. Paton mentioned in several places "the end of the missionary era." Other missionary writers and administrators have spoken likewise, or have used some similar phrase. Missionaries on furlough and some nationals from the overseas churches have also referred to the end of the missionary era.

One of the basic convictions expressed by Drs. Manikam and Thomas is that the missionary era has indeed come to an end—but that it coincides with, even overlaps, the beginning of the era of the churches. And they thank God for this development. So do I. As far back as my own days of field service in China (1917-28), I watched the steady progress away from a missionary-guided movement to a situation in which the Chinese became the district superintendents and bishops, assumed positions as heads of high schools, colleges, and hospitals. I realized how truly God-planned was such devolution. This realization became far more clear when, after the Japanese surrender in 1945, I went to China for several months of conference regarding postwar Christian work with National Christian Council and denominational groups. I found that the denominations that had advanced from mission-centered work to church-controlled life were already functioning well, while those that were still built upon mission control were waiting for the return of missionaries or for the coming to China of secretaries of boards of missions.

What was so evident to me in China in 1945 was even plainer when in late 1953 I visited briefly four of the countries of Southeast Asia. And it is with clear agreement that

I quote from Keith Bridston in his introduction to the recent book *Shock and Renewal*. He writes: "The end of the missionary era may have been brought in part by the sins and weaknesses of the missionary movement. But it was also brought by its strength. Therefore, it can be asserted that if the end of the missionary era is truly at hand, this may be seen as a sign of triumph and vindication for the missionary movement, for its ultimate aim has always been to make itself both unnecessary and dispensable."

But I would point out that the emerging church, and the scattered fragments of churches and church institutions, will doubtless operate in a continuing atmosphere of passionate nationalism, of international tensions, of economic difficulty and struggle, of resurgent religious ardor among non-Christians. There will be a time of frightening difficulties, even where illuminated by rays of strong hope. A clear statement of this Southeast Asian world today and tomorrow was made by the distinguished novelist, James A. Michener, at a dinner on October 5, 1955, given under the auspices of Fund for Asia, Inc. He described the Bandung Conference of the preceding summer, and he said:

An entire continent took the first strong steps forward in organizing itself for a successful future. The steps were not so sure as some Asian papers reported; they were not so well directed as some Asian leaders announced; and they were not so certain of success as all hoped. But they were of the greatest significance, because they were a good beginning toward the attainment of a strong, self-reliant continent.

But Mr. Michener did not leave us in any roseate glow of optimism. He has vision and hope, but he recognizes realities. In another connection, he said:

Although I saw enormous cause for optimism in Asia this summer, I am pessimistic about the immediate future. Too many problems remain unsettled. American attention in particular has been so focused on Geneva that we have overlooked the continued existence of every sore spot that troubled us so grievously last year. We are somewhat like the popular song: "If you dream hard enough, it will all come true." We seem about to enter an area where we shall have to contribute not only dreams but substantial work.

The Church in Southeast Asia is heartily commended alike to students of the Christian missionary movement, to those wanting to learn more about overseas missions, and to critics of Christian foreign missions. Probably I have read the manuscript more often and more critically than any other person, because the authors, resident overseas, agreed that I should abbreviate, rearrange, and where necessary rewrite the manuscript that represents so monumental a piece of research on their part. Out of such a background—friendship with the writers, familiarity with the churches in some of the areas treated, and intensive scrutiny of the manuscript—I recommend the prayerful study of the book. May it whet your mental appetite so that you will delve much deeper into the literature concerning Christianity in this highly important area. And may it help American Christians to focus more strongly and sympathetically their interest in, and their prayers for, the Christians in Southeast Asia.

FRANK T. CARTWRIGHT

New York, January, 1956

SOUTHEAST ASIA STATISTICS

THESE figures were prepared by the Far Eastern Joint Office of the National Council of Churches. In some cases, exact figures are unavailable, and the amounts given are approximate. The figures for Protestant Community include church members and non-members who worship with the Protestant groups.

COUNTRY	AREA SQ. MI.	POP. (MIL.)	PRINCIPAL RELIGION	PROTESTANT COMMUNITY
Burma	261,000	19	Buddhism	400,000
Taiwan (Formosa)	13,800	9.5	Buddhism	100,000
Indochina	286,000	27	Buddhism	70,000
Indonesia	906,000	78	Islam	5,000,000
Malaya	51,000	6.8	{ Islam { Buddhism	80,000
Philippines	115,600	21	Roman Catholicism	500,000
Thailand	200,000	19.5	Buddhism	30,000

CHAPTER 1

"Vast, Complex, Explosive"

Christianity is no newcomer to Asia. It was born in Asia. The ancient Syrian Church of Malabar, India, cherishes the belief that its founder was the Apostle Thomas. In the sixth century, Christians were worshiping in India and Ceylon. A hundred years later, when Christianity was first beginning to take root in England, the Christian gospel was carried to China by a Persian bishop. The Nestorian Church extended all the way from northern India to China during the early centuries of the Christian era.

The faith founded on Jesus Christ moved more slowly to the area of the world known today as Southeast Asia. By the sixteenth century, and even before, however, Christian missionaries were walking on the warm and fragrant shores lapped by the Indian Ocean.

This fact is not widely known among American Christians. Indeed, the entire area of Southeast Asia has been so far from the interests of most Americans that they would be pressed to give the names of nations found there.

The lands are Indonesia, the Philippine Islands, Burma, Malaya, Thailand, and Indochina. Immense as is the area they make up—almost two million square miles—the size is not the significant factor. Christianity does not deal with land masses; it is concerned with people. And people, old and young, are the best introduction to Southeast Asia.

LOOK AT THE PEOPLE

It is our good fortune that today we have increasingly better opportunities to become acquainted with Southeast Asians. We can see them on television and read about them in magazines and books. Some of us have heard their representatives in the United Nations or on the forum platforms in our own cities. They are interesting and attractive people, exotic in dress yet often speaking our language with a precision and musical quality that leads us humbly to wonder whether we could learn their languages as well as they have mastered ours.

There's danger in trying to make a generalization about the more than 180 million people of Southeast Asia. In dress, language, culture, and religion, they differ nation by nation, and within nations.

In the Philippines, for example, is a highly educated woman who is so attractive she would grace a gathering anywhere in the world. She stands before great meetings in the United States and speaks for the modern Filipinos with effectiveness and for Protestant Christianity with passion and conviction. Her personality has been tempered and her faith strengthened by suffering. Is there any wonder that she is influential throughout her own land and in ecumenical Christianity? Yet it would be foolish to take her as a typical example of a Filipina. We no more dare measure the population of the Philippine republic by such a woman than a Filipino would be safe in taking all Americans to be like the missionaries and Point IV workers who have lived and worked in his country. Many Filipinos are poorly dressed, often undernourished dwellers in *barrios* and small villages. The Republic of the Philippines is not an area to be studied; it is 21 million men and women and children, each one of them an individual, each created in the image of God.

Fifteen hundred miles to the west and south is Malaya. Among the Christians there is a man who would be outstanding in any country. From an ordinary home background, he entered a Christian school. Midway in his course of study, he was faced by the fact and call of Christ. He tested this Christianity and discovered, in his own words, that "It works! It *works!*" As he grew older, he won increasingly important positions in teaching and in administrative work, in local government, in world-wide Christian circles. Alert, friendly, devoted to young people, seeking ways in which to serve and influence his friends, he continues to bear witness that "It works."

In Burma, where Burmese and hill tribes and Chinese mingle in colorful human kaleidoscope, is a thin dynamo of a man who served his church members during all the hardships inflicted by World War II. Now in the difficult era of rehabilitation and of intense nationalism, he is constantly busy, working in churches, teaching school in shell-scarred buildings, administering simple clinics and baby-feeding stations. There is also a woman in the striking garb of her people, deeply Christian, keen of mind, concerned about the social and moral issues of government, at one time a member of the cabinet of her country.

Indonesia is a country struggling for national unity despite the thousands of islands that seem more like fragments of a nation than a unified whole. In Djakarta, in Makassar, in Medan—throughout the great archipelago—its people are carrying new responsibilities. Among them are Christians who have been drawn into governmental service or who are school administrators or teachers. The secretariat of the National Council of Churches requires able leadership, and churches depend on the guiding of their pastors. Likable, sensitive, idealistic yet at the same time practical, Indonesians are the kind of people who attract friendship.

LOOK AT THE LANDS

The Christian who is interested in the millions of human beings in Southeast Asia has to know something of the area's geography, climate, population, history, and culture. Above all, he is concerned with its Christians, the missionary efforts of the past, and the churches of the widely separated lands.

A good way to begin is with a look at a map. On the continent of Asia, beginning just south of China, are Burma and Indochina. Thailand rests between them, then farther to the south is Malaya, with Singapore, "the crossroads of Asia," at its tip. The rest of the immense area of Southeast Asia is made up of one vast reach of islands—Indonesia and the Philippines being the principal groups.

Both India and China have conditioned the area's total life for a thousand years. Their armies have overrun parts of Southeast Asia. Their merchants have controlled a large share of its commerce and trade. The religions have come primarily out of India, and Indian themes seem to dominate in the mixtures of Eastern and Western cultures that abound in the area.

The continental parts of Southeast Asia are predominantly Buddhist: Burma, Thailand, and much of Indochina. The island areas—Indonesia, the Malay Peninsula, and sections of Mindanao in the Philippines—are Muslim because of the penetration of Arab merchants.

Lying as it does, roughly between 30° north latitude and 10° south, Southeast Asia has a climate that is on the whole both hot and humid. Sea breezes temper the heat for much of the land, while some of the countries are favored with mountain areas, where well-to-do people can go for vacations away from the tropical heat.

Southeast Asia is primarily rural and agricultural; the life of the people is rooted in the soil. This does not mean they live like Kansas corn farmers or Wisconsin dairymen. The technological revolution in farming methods has influenced their mode of life even less than it has that of the people of Japan and India. Two types of agriculture are common: rice-growing on wet fields dominates the plains; in the hill country, crops sprout from ground cleared by burning.

The people of Southeast Asia generally favor some form of economic socialism. Private capital to finance industries scarcely exists. Thus there can be no extensive building of industrial plants unless governments are prepared to pay for it. A cabinet member of one of the younger governments said, "Free enterprise as the West knows it is something we Asians cannot afford."

Racially, linguistically, and culturally, the peoples are a babel. Some of them represent ancient and impressive cultures, as evidenced by the ruins of Borobudor and Angkor.

The Thai, Malay, Cambodian, Burmese, and Annamese are the major races, but their blood streams and destinies have been conditioned by Chinese and Mongoloid immigrants from the north, and by Dravidians, Hindus, and Arabs from the West. The Dutch have claimed by way of justifying their retention of Western New Guinea (Irian) that the Indonesians and Irianians are different peoples. Yet the original stocks of Irian may also be found in Timor, Sumatra, Malaya, the Philippines, and as far west as Ceylon. The Indonesian nation itself includes at least five distinct racial groups, and some of these people can be taken for members of the present dominant peoples of Irian.

CHANGING PATTERNS OF GOVERNMENT

Self-government is still a new fact to most of the peoples of Southeast Asia. In Malaya and Indochina, it is still a dream of the future. In the Philippines and to a lesser extent in Burma, peoples now independent were tutored for the responsibilities of freedom. Indonesians won their liberty without great experience in self-government.

The tidal emotions that sweep Southeast Asia cannot be understood unless it is remembered that, with only one exception, all of the countries concerned have been colonies of Western nations. The exception is Thailand. The others have been subject to the West—Malaya and Burma under British rule, Indochina under French, Indonesia under Dutch, and the Philippines first under Spanish and then American domination. Malaya and parts of Borneo and New Guinea are still colonial in nature.

Japanese conquest in World War II was a historical watershed for this area. The relations between conqueror and conquered differed from nation to nation, but the three years of Japanese rule had two results common to all the area: an accentuated move toward freedom and the loss of some degree of internal peace and stability. In the Philippines, Indonesia, Malaya, and Burma, Japan played the part of liberator in overthrowing Western colonial power. Thailand capitulated early and declared war on the Allies.

The Japanese set up the first Indonesian-led government in Indonesia in centuries and trained some of the men who since have given the nation leadership in its first days as a republic. A puppet regime was established also in the Philippines, yet more than one million Filipinos claimed that they fought as guerrillas against the Japanese. Ten years have not been enough to overcome their bitterness toward Japan.

Burmans who had been anti-British cooperated with the Japanese in setting up a cooperative government. Like other Southeast Asians, they discovered that Japan's liberation was liberation in name only.

In Indochina, Japanese worked through French officials cooperating with the Axis powers. When defeat became imminent, the French were ousted and the government was staffed with the people of the country. Indochina's position today might have been significantly different had these leaders been in power for three years instead of one.

Malaya was the single area that was not promised eventual independence by the Japanese. Japan simply replaced Great Britain as the colonial power and enforced the will of Nippon upon the regional sultans.

The problems of keeping peace and order in the new republics today are made more difficult by the peoples' experiences with firearms and guerrilla activities during the occupation. It was the Chinese, actively persecuted by the Japanese in Malaya, who organized resistance and received arms from the Allies. Some of the same men, Communist-led, put this training to use when they launched the revolt in September, 1949. In Indonesia, the armies of Dar'ul Islam, intransigents who refused to abide by the cease fire agreements during the struggle between the infant republic and the Dutch, have continued to embarrass the Djakarta government, particularly in West Java and on the island of Celebes. The anarchy that developed in Burma under the Japanese continued under new labels against the free Burman government. In Indochina, the attempts of the French to reassert their authority after Japan's defeat developed into a series of tragic events that brought death to thousands of people and the gradual growth of Communist influence.

RELIGIOUS NATIONALISM

One of the significant features of Southeast Asia politics today is the use of religion as a basis for nationalism. A country in Southeast Asia does not have unity because of geography or because the people speak the same language; what unifies a country is the people's common cultural and spiritual heritage. Thus national leaders are interested in restoring ancient faiths to full glory. In Burma, pagodas are built and festivals are encouraged to re-establish the power of Buddhism. In Indonesia, Islam is being revived.

Religious nationalism poses two serious problems to Christian communities. One is that the strongest religious group in a country might gain a monopoly of social and economic privileges. The other is that such a strong body might persuade the state to ban or limit Christian evangelism.

In brief, since World War II there has been no return to the old *status quo* in Southeast Asia—save possibly in Thailand.

POLITICAL CHANGES AND THE CHURCH

Political developments have strongly affected the life and work of the churches in the area. Japanese occupation made it necessary for Southeast Asian Christians to conduct the churches' business without the counsel of Western missionaries. For more than three years, the churches were isolated from their former mission bases. Consequently they had to become self-governing and self-supporting. Christians had to hold to their faith against persecution in Burma and Thailand. Buddhists victimized them; they were not permitted to hold civil service positions. Muslims in some parts of Indonesia did likewise, with the blessing of the Japanese Army. The treatment accorded Christians in a given area depended in large measure upon the attitude of the particular Japanese officer in command. Christians in South Borneo (Kalimantan) reported that the Christian minister attached to the Japanese Army of occupation obtained subsidies for Christian work, but on the island of Timor, Christians were persecuted and meeting places closed.

None of the churches have returned to the old relationships that existed with missions before the war. The autonomy they enjoyed under the Japanese, even though accompanied by hardships and suffering, they largely have retained. The partnership that has emerged between churches and mission bodies is the goal that has been implicit in missionary strategy since the beginning.

These churches—of many denominations, some of which

are rent by regional or other schisms—are at one and the same time the bulwark of Christianity in Southeast Asia and the sharp edge of Christian advance. But we must remind ourselves continually of what these churches are. They are more than institutions; they are people—human beings who have been caught up in loyalty to Jesus Christ as he is embodied in his church. They are people who express that loyalty more or less perfectly in what they conceive to be the work of the church.

It is these young churches that, above all else in the vast, complex, and explosive area where they are witnessing, demand the interest, the concern, and the prayers of fellow Christians throughout the world.

CHAPTER 2

Churches, Missions, and Missionaries

Churches that are completely Asian in pastors and people are the new significant fact in the missionary movement in Southeast Asia. In a limited sense, these churches are to American and European mission groups what the young governments of Asia are to the Western nations that once were colonial powers. They are to be treated as equals, even as Western governments must treat the administrations of newly established states. Of course, such a comparison is inadequate in at least one way. It ignores the bonds of love that are so important in Christian relations and so neglected in international relations.

The older churches of the West can do only those things in Asia requested by the sister churches of the East. A sort of ecumenical paradox arises at this point: Church mission boards that gave birth to, or nurtured, Asian churches must recognize their rights and responsibilities. There are Western sects, on the other hand, who send out missionaries with little regard for the wishes and agreements of other Christians—Western and Asian.

Strong practical reasons still link Asian churches to the

West. The churches of Southeast Asia do not have enough trained people to preach the gospel to the unsaved and un-churched. They lack the resources of money and personnel to spread the Christian community. They must be rein-forced with technical assistance and funds if they are to do the job mission work is intended to do.

PAST CONTRIBUTIONS OF MISSIONS

What is this job? In each of the lands of Asia, the first mis-sionaries followed a common pattern of operations and had a common aim. Through education, medicine, and preach-ing of the Word, they sought to influence the maximum number of people to accept Christ as Lord and Saviour, and of these converts to form a church that would eventually support and govern itself and reach others for Christ.

One of the very earliest of the adventuresome men who helped open Southeast Asia to Christianity was Francis Xavier. In the sixteenth century, he appeared on the coast of Malaya, teaching and evangelizing. Before he moved on to the farther reaches of the Orient, he established the be-ginnings of Roman Catholicism in the area.

Early in the nineteenth century, Adoniram Judson, an American and an individualist of high order, started for Asia as part of a team from the American Board of Com-missioners for Foreign Missions. On his way over, he felt that he was led to become a Baptist and that he was responsible for planting Baptist missions in Burma. During his decades of service in the land of pagodas, he was the center of Chris-tian work. As one of his colleagues said, "Judson *was* the Burma mission."

A hundred years earlier, when the Dutch became the

dominant power in the East Indies, their ships carried missionaries to that area. The records of those early days tell of strong individuals who went their ways as they felt the Spirit of God leading them.

One more example, from more recent times. In the first years of this century, hundreds of Christian Chinese migrated to Sarawak because of the Boxer Rebellion. A Methodist missionary named James Hoover followed them, and for most of the next three decades, he and his wife were the only missionaries, and at no time were there more than two others in the entire area.

In most of the lands of Southeast Asia, however, the work of individual missionaries was soon supported by the establishment of a mission. This was—and in some areas still is—the method by which distant boards of missions in Europe or North America administer their work. The mission made all major decisions regarding Christian work in its area; it was dominated by Western missionaries.

SHIFTING OF CONTROL

Such domination could not last forever. Even before the growth of today's nationalism, missionaries of foresight realized that there must be a shift from mission control to control by the Christians of Asia.

Writing more than thirty years ago about the progress of the gospel, a missionary contrasted the meager missionary beginnings in Siam (now Thailand) in 1867 with the results a half century later. The results included hundreds of students in self-supporting Christian schools and thousands of patients being treated each year in Christian hospitals. Siamese pastors, evangelists, and teachers were many times more numerous than the Western staff. Because these developments came gradually, the church was able to carry on under the Japanese occupation in World War II. The congregation sent laymen into villages to preach to those beyond the reach of established churches.

In Burma in 1853, the Karens financed and opened work in Bassein, just twenty-five years after the first Karen convert had been baptized. Later some of them declared their independence of the mission. The mission felt all effort should be concentrated on evangelism, while the Sgaw Karens desired educational activities also. For thirteen years, they maintained their independence, a fact that has contributed largely to their self-reliance over the years. Today, the Sgaw Karens are about three fourths Christianized, whereas the Pwo Karen Christians, who did not enjoy the period of independent activity, are fewer in comparison with their people's total number. A statesman of Burma, Senator Shwe Ba, said of the experience, "Rowing against the stream makes for strength. That may be what we need now."

The magnificent spirit of Karen Christianity is expressed in words put down by the Thra S'Peh, a Bassein Karen. Of the Kachin people in Bhamo, to whom he carried the gospel in 1886, he wrote:

I pity this people very much. They want very much to learn, but at present I am all alone on the mountains among them. Owing to fighting among Kachins and Burmese, I cannot travel freely. . . . The Burmese have announced that they would massacre all Kachins of fifteen and upwards. . . . Teacher Cushing told me if the Burmese attacked one mountain, to flee to the next. . . . I am ready to cast my lot with these poor

Kachins, to suffer with them, and to lead them with my whole heart to Christ, as Moses cast in his lot with the children of Israel.

The necessity for achieving self-support was made sharp and clear in most lands by the Japanese invasion in late 1941 and early 1942. War broke contacts between the churches and their Western supporters, forcing the young churches to look after themselves or perish. Said the leader of the Church of Minahassa (the extreme northeastern tip of Celebes, to the south of Mindanao), "Prior to the coming of the Japanese, we had discussed self-support. After the Japanese came, we had to do something about it." In some few instances, Japanese churches gave assistance, but generally, the Southeast Asian church bodies had to go it alone.

NEW RELATIONSHIPS BETWEEN MISSION AND CHURCH

The shift from mission to church followed two major patterns. In some areas and by some Western sending agencies, the mission is still continuing as an administrating group. Church and mission develop side by side, the former dealing with ecclesiastical matters, the latter receiving and disbursing funds from the Western churches, dividing the money between the church and its educational, medical, or social institutions. In other areas, the mission has gradually disappeared, the missionaries serving as administrators only by virtue of membership in the Asian church and upon election by their colleagues. Financial, as well as ecclesiastical matters, are dealt with by the church, usually through a central committee appointed by the church.

A mere change in the man at the reins doesn't make a wagon out of a buggy. A major fact—and problem—in the life of Asian churches is that missionaries, subsidized by Western churches, used methods that Asian churches can't afford. Schools that provide both general education and technical training for Christian leaders still are needed, but if the church in Asia is to support them, appeals must be made to non-Christians or to the state for money. Christian hospitals can free themselves of foreign support only by obtaining government backing or by catering to people in middle-class and upper income brackets. Yet one of the Christian contributions has been making medical services available to those unable to pay. Local churches, with full-time pastors, are themselves a drain upon the economy of Asian lands, particularly the small groups that comprise the Evangelical communities. Self-support is possible in several lands only if ministers supplement their earnings by teaching, farming, or some other part-time work.

In short, self-government was achieved in most Asian churches before self-support. The demand for national independence encouraged a demand for ecclesiastical independence. The technical term "devolution" is generally used to indicate the gradual process whereby authority and control were transferred by missionaries to the people they had served. Responsibility for preaching and pastoral work was first to go, since this was the task easiest for Asians to perform and hardest for Western missionaries. The exceptions to this general rule have been university churches and city churches with a high proportion of intellectuals. Medical and educational responsibilities have been transferred. Theological education has been the activity in which missionary influence has lasted longest. Possibly this is because trained Asians who are needed as teachers are even more needed in the life of the churches.

First there was the individual missionary. The mission was a logical and necessary development. And now the Christian missionary movement has reached its fullest expression in the churches.

CHAPTER 3

The Churches of Southeast Asia

M r. and Mrs. Jorge Quismundo, the young
and attractive couple who were the first Filipino missionaries to serve in Indonesia, attended a Reformation Day
service one day. Held on an Indonesian football field, it
brought together Protestants of several persuasions. All of
them were gripped by the spirit of the occasion. The climax
came at the end of the program when, while many non-
Christians watched them, the Protestants joined in song. A
tropical rain storm was pelting down but could not smother
the voices that sang, in Malay, Martin Luther's great hymn,
"A Mighty Fortress Is Our God."

The incident reveals a great deal that is true of church
life in Southeast Asia. The picture is one of variety in organization and method, yet one of growing unity in spirit.

DIFFERENCES IN CHURCH FORMS

A person traveling from one country to another discov-
ers marked differences in worship and church organization.
Many of these differences were originally imported from
the West. They were brought by the missionaries who,

being loyal Baptists or Presbyterians or Anglicans, gave converts the beliefs and the mold of church organization that they knew. Consequently, Southeast Asian churches show denominational patterns, sometimes half-heartedly, sometimes with strong loyalty.

A visitor who notes these differences created by Western influence will find other differences that have sprung from the cultures of Asia. Languages and customs set people apart. Among the Karens of Upper Burma, in the long-house worship of Borneo's Dyak Christians, in the Philippines and Thailand and elsewhere, he will come upon elements in the church life that are quite dissimilar. For the most part, these are minor differences, but they tend to keep the churches somewhat apart. Many missionaries have observed that, as the educational level of the Christians rises, and especially as they travel and participate in ecumenical assemblies, some of the differences tend to disappear. The same observers, however, also point out that Western-implanted differences persist longer and, outwardly at least, with greater vigor.

BONDS IN WORSHIP

For all the varied ways in which the Christians of Southeast Asia conduct their church affairs, many strong bonds exist between them, and when seen in the light cast by the many likenesses, the differences recede into relative unimportance. These Christians share a common allegiance to Christ as Lord and Master, a fairly uniform set of beliefs with which they can confront Islam, Buddhism, Hinduism, and animism, and a general pattern of operational methods and aims.

What are some of the common elements found among the Christians and churches of Southeast Asia?

Practically every congregation makes use of singing. It may sound primitive and unharmonious to Western ears, but it affords spiritual expression for the singers. In the heart of a Sumatran jungle, after traveling far from the city by decrepit auto, then for part of a day on foot with half-naked guides leading through nearly impassable growth, we found a Christian congregation. We worshiped with them for two hours and then went to bed—but not to sleep. Until after midnight, those Bataks sang "the songs of Zion," some familiar to us, others unknown.

The music is frequently of high quality. Anyone who has ever traveled on Sunday among the many strong churches of the Toba Plateau has heard those Indonesians sing European music so difficult that many American congregations would hesitate to try it. In cities throughout Southeast Asia —Manila, Djakarta, Singapore, Medan, and Rangoon, for example—choirs of splendid singers add stateliness to worship services.

The use of the Bible in the languages of the people is common to all the churches of the area we are concerned with. Protestants must have access to the Word of God and in scores, even hundreds of languages, the Word is in the hands of myriad congregations. Many churches place Bibles in the pews, both for congregational reading aloud and to enable the worshipers to follow the preachers' reading.

The need for the printed Bible has demanded the attention of missionaries and of native scholars. Translation and revision have been necessary. And if, as is still true in parts of Southeast Asia, the language has not yet been reduced to writing, this must be done in order that the Bible and other books of worship can be prepared.

An Indonesian Bible translator has recalled that, though he was a Simalungen Batak, the Bible used in the church where he worshiped as a child was Toba Batak. Thus he grew up thinking that Jesus was of the other tribal group. When later the Bible was produced in the language of the Simalungen Bataks, the spiritual life of his people was deepened.

The Kachin Bible is another example. Missionary Ola Hanson had first to learn the spoken language, then reduce it to writing. This task took four years. In sixteen years, he prepared a dictionary, hymnal, and other texts. Finally, after twenty-six years, he had produced a translation of the complete Bible in Kachin.

Another common factor among Christian groups is worship. This has been implied in the mention of music and the use of the Bible, but it should be made explicit. No matter where you go in this entire region, wherever you find Christian groups you find them engaged in some form of worship. It may be, and often is, simple in the extreme. The lay leader or the preacher may have no knowledge of the niceties of worship. At the other extreme, you may find stately, even "high church," ritual presided over by men in clerical robes.

THE CHURCHES AND EDUCATION

For the most part, the churches of Southeast Asia stress education. Respect for education among most Asian people, coupled in areas under British control with the educational policy of training civil servants, affected the beginnings of the churches' educational policies. In the Philippines, educational policies and methods reflect both Spanish and American influences.

Critics of the churches' achievements in education assert that, with a few notable exceptions, the education is the kind that produces a "white collar" class. Clerks have been needed in civil service and in business; education was an open door to such positions, highly esteemed in nearly all Southeast Asia. Generally speaking, the products of this type of education have not met Asia's demand for men and women skilled in the crafts, professions, agriculture, and technology.

Whatever the achievements and shortcomings, education sponsored by missions has provided men and women capable of church leadership. The schools have graduated thousands of persons with at least some knowledge of Christian principles. Many of them are staunch followers of Jesus Christ. In Burma in 1954, the Baptists reported 31,612 pupils in schools entirely supported and governed by the Christian groups. Methodists in Malaya stress education, operating 62 schools with 42,505 students enrolled. Fifteen hundred primary schools and 159 middle schools are under church auspices in Indonesia. In the Philippines, 52 schools of the Association of Christian Schools and Colleges reported an enrollment of 17,000 for 1954-55. In Thailand the reported enrollment is also 17,000. There are no Protestant schools in Indochina.

THE CHURCHES AND HEALTH

Another emphasis of Christianity in Southeast Asia is on hospital care and health education. An Asian social worker-pastor said that he conducts a medical clinic because "This is where the God of love about whom I preach comes alive to the people." The McCormick Hospital in Chiengmai, the Mary Johnston Hospital in Manila, the Bethesda Hospital in Djokjakarta (Java), the Ellen Mitchell Memorial Hospital in Moulmein—these and other Christian hospitals set an example of medical skill and efficiency for government and private institutions to aim at. Their staffs combine the medical profession's desire to serve humanity with the selfless motivation of the Christian faith.

Small though the Christian community is in Southeast Asia, its witness through the ministry of healing has been powerful. Some Christian doctors have set up practice in rural areas and economically retarded districts, even though working conditions are bad and the income low. A Burmese Christian resigned her government post to accept a position in a Christian institution at a greatly reduced salary. She wanted to make a Christian contribution to the national health campaign. Christian teachers, evangelists, and preaching missionaries, utilizing their elementary knowledge of hygiene and armed with simple household remedies, have taken healing to isolated areas which no skilled practitioner has ever before visited.

Churches have been forced to concern themselves with conditions that endanger the physical well-being of people. Malaria, for example, is a major problem in every land of Southeast Asia. In Burma, two fifths of all deaths are caused by it. Everyone—from farmers to theological students—expects to be ill a certain number of days each year from malaria. Tuberculosis is another killer in Asia, even as it is in the West. Diet deficiencies weaken human resistance to disease. The tempo of educational life in Asian schools demands more energy than the traditional diet supplies. Flies, lack of ice to preserve foods, uncovered foods in the markets, absence of sanitary facilities in the cities—all contribute to the prevalence of stomach ailments and are among the factors that keep life expectancy low.

Church hospitals thus work both in the fields of preventive medicine and of public health. Thirteen hospitals in Thailand, founded by the missions, are related to the Church of Christ. In the past, European missions, in cooperation with colonial governments of the East Indies, established more than forty large hospitals and hundreds of clinics throughout the islands. Protestant hospitals were established in the Philippines following an older tradition established by the Roman Catholic missionaries. A pattern has developed over the years: Missions make people health conscious; governments supplement mission work; finally government institutions replace church agencies and Christian medical work disappears, or remains an incidental experiment.

CHRISTIANITY AND THE STATUS OF WOMEN

There is another characteristic of church life in Southeast Asia that is of a different sort than the ones mentioned so far. Generally, the status of women has been raised wherever the church has taken root. This is both because Christianity accords women equality with men and because education offered by Christian agencies has enabled women to develop their abilities—and to assert their rights.

This generalization cannot be uniformly applied. Women in some countries of this area were indeed held down, but even in pre-British days, Burman women did not regard their interests as being different or separate from those of

men. Being equal with men in respect to property owner-
ship, divorce, business, and inheritance, they had substantial status. In the Philippines, women reflect the more than
three centuries of Spanish and American influence. They
retain much that is feminine, but participate vigorously in
government, education, and business.

Yet even in lands where the level of women's life was
highest, Christianity has raised that level. Literacy is more
widespread among Christian women than among non-
Christian in even the more advanced countries of Southeast
Asia. The postwar extension of wider political rights to
women found Christian women ready for responsible posts.
Kua Saligupta of Thailand vividly illustrates this fact. The
daughter of a high official who was a Buddhist, she gained
her primary and higher education through church influence.
Her ability and her devotion have brought high recognition
for her in the Christian educational system of Thailand.

In the Philippines, a Protestant woman, Mrs. Ascunsion
A. Perez, has served as a member of the cabinet. During the
early years of Burma's national development, a Protestant
woman, Mrs. Ba Maung Chain, was likewise a minister in the
government. Women have been elected to the legislature
in Burma since before World War II; Indonesian women are
members of the national Parliament. Two women were ordained by the Protestant church in 1954, the first Indonesian
women to be given full rights in the ministry.

MOVEMENT TOWARD UNITY

Typical also of Christianity in Southeast Asia is a trend
toward unity and world-wide church contacts. Movement
toward unity was accelerated during the Japanese occupa-

tion, both under duress and for mutual protection. In Burma, as an example, the churches found it possible and advisable to cooperate. While no united church has resulted, the joint activities of the churches through the Burmese Christian Council and associated organizations have been greatly increased since the war.

There long has been only the Church of Christ in Thailand, which now embraces the activities of three foreign mission agencies, American Presbyterians, American Baptists, and British Disciples. The many groups that have entered Thailand since the closing of war generally have been cooperative, and many have worked according to agreements that prevent overlapping of efforts.

The Indonesian Council of Churches was formed in 1950 for the sole stated purpose of effecting a single united church of Christ in the archipelago. While no immediate organic realization of this aim is in sight, numerous other joint services and activities have developed.

The United Church of Christ in the Philippines includes approximately one half the Protestants. The largest other group is Methodist. Both of these have worked together through the Philippine Federation of Christian Churches, engaging jointly in such activities as audio-visual work, production of literature, and conferences. The next chapter provides a closer look at this work and the intriguing country where it is going on.

CHAPTER 4

The Philippine Islands

Of all the lands in Southeast Asia, best known in the United States are the islands annexed by this country in 1898, following the Spanish-American War. The seizure was in conformity with the then popular pattern of colonialism. Democratic principles triumphed, however, and the Philippines and the United States embarked upon a program of conscious development toward complete political autonomy for the islands.

The American occupation was preceded by 333 years of Spanish rule. Before the coming of the Spaniards, the islanders were already trading with Japan and China. Spain developed that commerce, extending operations to Mexico. Under the Spanish, more than 70 per cent of the people became Roman Catholics, a development that is without parallel in any of the other colonies of Asia.

During that long period, the Filipinos had risen against Spain approximately each quarter century. All uprisings had been quelled until that of 1896, inspired by José Rizal, one of the greatest men produced in any era of Philippine history. His gifts were ideological and spiritual. Ultimately he was arrested by the Spaniards and was shot. But the revolt lived. He was the forerunner of the entire group of Malayan anticolonial revolutionaries.

The struggle of the Filipinos against the United States, begun in February of 1898, ended three years later with the American promise of independence for the Philippines. Each decade autonomy was extended, until the proclamation of independence July 4, 1946.

The Japanese occupation of the islands in World War II proved that the Filipinos had learned the lessons of democracy well. They did not accept the slogans of the Japanese, and they set up guerrilla forces that fought behind the Japanese lines until the war's end. But an aftermath of this resistance, as in other countries, was an army that remained to oppose the new republic.

The Huk (shortened form of Hukbalahap) revolt, which was centered mostly in Central Luzon and which sorely tried the many skills of President Ramón Magsaysay, while patently Communist led, was fed not so much by Marxian dialectic as by popular dissatisfaction. Corruption in government, poverty, and landlordism drove Filipinos to join the Huk forces. Evicted farmers, unemployed workers, defeated politicians, bored village youths, and disillusioned idealists abandoned ballots for bullets, seeking to secure justice. So serious was the rebel movement that the restoration of peace and order became the government's top priority. Magsaysay's settlement of the Huk uprising by working toward a solution of the economic and psychological causes of dissatisfaction at the same time that government troops were meeting force with force was highly successful.

Regionalism is strong, almost necessarily so. More than

eighty languages are used by the 21 million people. The 7,100 islands cover 115,707 square miles of land, an area about the size of Arizona, but they are stretched out over an expanse as far as from Chicago to New Orleans, and from Kansas City to Cleveland. About 23 per cent of the land area is under cultivation.

Most of Asia is at least suspicious of the United States. Some of the peoples are openly hostile. Yet, among the Filipinos there is much praise, little criticism toward the United States, despite trade agreements that give this country an economic advantage and despite a peace treaty with Japan that Filipinos feel makes Japan the real victor in the Pacific war. Filipino friendliness means that military bases are available to the United States. Voice of America programs to other parts of Asia are relayed from Manila. The Filipino contingent in the UN Army in Korea was second in size only to that of the United States.

Compared with other colonial powers, the United States has been generous to the Philippines. Political independence was given freely rather than having to be seized by revolt. Filipinos were trained to assume governmental responsibilities. A school system was established, so extensive that today one person in five out of the 21 million is studying in an educational institution. Highways and communications were developed. English became an official language.

But some of the Philippine problems are a consequence of American lavishness. The poverty, governmental corruption, economic feudalism, and sense of insecurity upon which communism feeds and grows are no worse in the Philippines than elsewhere in Asia. But they appear worse to the Filipino people because America has set such high standards. A Manila University student said, "Americans are responsible for our predicament. They have come here in their fast cars and made us want them. In their movies, they have shown us a kind of life we want for ourselves. But they have not given us the means of achieving that kind of life."

THE PEOPLE OF THE ISLANDS

People of Malay stock constitute 90 per cent or more of the inhabitants. The Chinese, the second largest population group, have been in commercial contact with the islands possibly since before the Malay invasions and constantly thereafter. While the population of "pure" Chinese stock is less than 200,000, the intermarriage of Chinese men and Filipina women has produced a group of mixed blood called *Mestizo Chino*. They are competent, strong people, many of whom have risen to national leadership. Filipino national hero, José Rizal, "Pride of the Malay," had at least one Chinese ancestor. Some of the presidents have had Chinese blood.

The early Malay settlers found small black people, similar to the inhabitants of New Guinea and the Australian aborigines. They have been reduced in numbers through intermarriage and wars and are found today only in the mountain places. They were never converted to Islam or Roman Catholicism. They are listed today as pagan.

The Malays who occupied the islands were of the same stock as those found in Indonesia and Malaya. Their linguistic differences are assumed to derive from their having emigrated from different islands. The Visayans number almost one half of the Filipinos. About one quarter are Tagalogs. The remainder are Ilokanos, Bikols, Pampangos, and Pangasinans. One of the strange features of national life is that Tagalog is the official national language.

The Moros in Mindanao are Islamic. They have more in common culturally with Indonesia than with the Philippines. This historical connection is potentially a significant factor in the future relations between the two young republics. The Moros were never conquered by the Spaniards. They were a frequent source of irritation to the United States during the American rule. Their homeland is now claiming the attention of Manila. The Moros live in only three of the nine provinces on Mindanao, the majority of the population on this island as elsewhere in the Philippines being Roman Catholic or Evangelical.

Magsaysay initiated a resettlement project whereby landless farmers and dissidents in overcrowded Luzon could homestead their own fields in Mindanao. Certain long neglected developments have resulted and will result. The Methodist Church followed those among its own members who were in the migration of landless peasants to the South. Mindanao also is the island to which Indonesian immigrants have come to engage in seasonal agricultural jobs. The unregulated nature of this migrant flow has forced the two governments to formulate procedures and establish check points between Mindanao and Celebes.

Educationally the Philippines stand highest in Southeast Asia. Most of this advance was made under United States' tutelage, though the University of Santo Tomas, where many Americans were interned by the Japanese during World War II, was founded under the Spanish in the seventeenth century.

Beginning in 1900, public schools were opened. American soldiers served as the first teachers. One year later, a thousand teachers arrived on a single transport. Today, nearly five million Filipinos are enrolled in schools. This is the highest ratio in the world outside the United States.

The educational pattern has been influenced by its American founders and is divided into three units: elementary, high school, and college. The use of English as the medium of instruction has resulted in English becoming the language of the educated, although regional languages are still used outside the schools. While the Islands still are crippled because of the destruction wrought by military occupation and liberation, a large proportion of reconstruction funds have been allocated to the rebuilding of educational plants.

Commercialized education is an ill consequence of the desire of Filipino youth for degrees. Hundreds of colleges, high schools, and universities have developed since the war in response to the clamor for educational opportunities. One of these is alleged to have declared a 100 per cent dividend to the stockholders in one year. It is not unusual for a single person to be "president" of several schools. A prominent Manila citizen, who is not primarily an educator, is head of more than a dozen schools and "colleges."

Law is the most popular subject, for while it is true that technological education in Asia is lagging, it is also true that Asian youth in general and Filipino youth in particular would rather major in jurisprudence, which prepares for a government career, than to train for such shirt-sleeve occupations as engineering or farming.

The former Minister of Private Education justified the lax educational program indicated above as a means of producing needed teachers. By letting down the educational bars, he sought to train sufficient leaders, including teachers, to meet the Islands' needs.

THE CHURCH

The country in East Asia with the largest number of Christians is the Philippines, with a population of 21 million, of whom about 17 million are Christians. A little over a million belong to the animistic mountain races. In some of the islands there are Muslims, but the bulk of the people are Christians. Of the 17 million Christians, 15 million belong to the Roman Catholic Church, one and a half million to the Philippine Independent (Aglipayan) Church, and one half million to the Protestant churches. It should be noted that the Protestant figure covers only adults; Roman Catholic and Aglipayan statistics include children.

Roman Catholic influence in the land is traditional and strong. Ancient churches and cathedrals dot the landscape. But there is also a strong tradition of opposition to the Roman Catholic hierarchy, and in particular to its foreign priests. The vigorous Protestant minority has stirred the Roman Catholic Church to action, and as a result, Bible reading, youth conferences, and social action are now being promoted by that church. At the same time, Roman Catholic opposition to the Protestant church is on the increase, as is evidenced by its threat to excommunicate Catholics who join the Y.M.C.A. or who send their children to Protestant schools.

The Philippine Independent Church, popularly known as the Aglipayan Church, broke away from Rome in 1902 under the leadership of Father Gregorio Aglipay and Don

Isabelo de los Reyes. The Aglipayan Church repudiated papal authority, permitted its clergy to marry, and introduced the vernacular languages into the services. Today, it has little inner cohesion; both Evangelical and Roman Catholic churches draw from it. While its ministerial candidates are trained at St. Andrew's Seminary of the Episcopal Church in the Philippines, it has not joined the Philippine Federation of Christian Churches and can not be classified as either Roman Catholic or Evangelical.

The development of the Evangelical churches from no membership in 1898 to a community embracing 2.4 per cent of the total population is a rate of growth without parallel in any other Asian land. This small Protestant community in the Philippines is far more influential than its numbers would indicate. Most of the social workers in the country are Protestants. Evangelical Christians are playing an increasingly important role in the nation's life; the fourteen hundred ministers of the Protestant churches are comparatively well trained, thanks to Union Theological Seminary in Manila, the Baptist Seminary at Iloilo, St. Andrew's in Manila, and the Silliman University College of Theology. Christian education is of a fairly high order, especially in view of the fact that education in the Philippines is so highly commercialized. Silliman University has a high reputation and ranks along with the University of the Philippines. The Baptist Central Philippine University at Iloilo serves a large area in the South.

Christianity in the Philippines may be illustrated by introducing one among the many great leaders of the Evangelical church in that land. A saintly, modest man named Proculo A. Rodriguez is one of the most highly regarded leaders of the United Church of Christ in the Philippines. His fellow Christians learned long ago that behind Dr. Rodriguez' unassuming manner is a record of devoted and fruitful Christian service.

Before he was given charge of United Church activities in the Mindanao area, his accomplishments in religious education had led to his appointment as director of the Extension Service of Silliman University. The Extension Service reaches out a helping hand to people in rural areas. It brings assistance and advice on agriculture, health, education, citizenship, and religion.

"Most of our efforts are church-centered, but with the aim to serve the community," Dr. Rodriguez said of the Extension Service. "We keep it clear in our own minds and to the people that only through the spirit of Christ can permanent social welfare be achieved."

Dr. Rodriguez' slight figure has inspired confidence in harsher climates than those of classroom and pulpit. During World War II, he was pastor of a rugged area of the interior of Negros and guided his people through the Japanese occupation and the sometimes heavy-handed, light-fingered rule of guerrilla forces. Today there is a line of Protestant churches throughout that area as a result of Dr. Rodriguez' work.

The United Church of Christ in the Philippines is a union of Presbyterian, U.S.A., Congregational-Christian, Evangelical, United Brethren, and Philippine Independent Methodist churches, and about half of the Disciples of Christ churches. The Methodist Church that is related to the American Methodist Board of Missions is outside this union. The United Church of Christ and the Methodist Church are the two largest Protestant churches in the country. The Methodist Church's strength is in Luzon, north of Manila. The UCCP strength generally lies south.

The Methodist Church has a membership of 75,000 and a total community of 106,000. The UCCP membership is 96,261 with a community of 230,000. Splits from larger bodies are impelled not by theological or doctrinal differences but by nationalistic motives, personality tensions, and also because of individual power possibilities in a sectarian development. The UNIDA (Iglesia Evangelica Unida de Cristo) has a membership of 15,000, with three times this number within its total community. IEMELIF (Iglesia Evangelica Metodista en las Islas Filipinas) has a membership of 25,000 and a community of almost three times this size. These bodies are members of the Philippine Federation of Christian Churches and cooperate with the parent churches in joint projects.

The Convention of Philippine Baptist Churches, also part of the Federation, is affiliated with the American Baptist Foreign Mission Society. Most of the Philippine Baptist churches are located on Panay and nearby islands. The membership of 20,000 is the nucleus of a community of 50,-000. Other Baptist groups are making inroads upon their operations. The Conservative Baptist Foreign Mission Society, the Southern Baptist Convention, and the World Fundamental Baptist Missionary Fellowship (U.S.A.) have made beginnings. The Association of Baptists for World Evangelism has 6,500 members and a community of 25,000. The Seventh-Day Adventists have a membership of 35,000, a community of 75,000.

The Protestant Episcopal Church works primarily among

the American residents and conducts a mission to the pagans of the mountains, the Igorots, and other tribes. Communicants number more than 11,000. The Episcopal community is estimated at 30,000.

A total of twenty-five American societies, one British, one internationally supported, and ten national church bodies are making the Protestant approach. Here as elsewhere, this multiplicity of organization releases a larger number of workers to an area, but it is confusing to non-Christians and to young Protestants to be presented with such a diversity of doctrines, often by representatives who engage in recrimination.

In spite of the rapid growth of Protestant denominations in the Philippines, the Philippine Federation of Christian Churches plays an important role in church life. It corresponds to the National Christian Councils in other countries, with the important difference that only churches (and not missions) are members of the Federation. The Federation serves a useful function in bringing the smaller independent groups into a cooperative relationship with the Methodists and the UCCP. A Federation student center has been erected on the campus of the University of the Philippines. Among cooperative efforts should also be listed a strong and active Y.M.C.A. and a smaller but influential Y.W.C.A.

The church in the Philippines has become missionary minded. In 1952, the UCCP held a large number of institutes to study the churches in Indonesia, as a result of which they have sent out a Filipino missionary couple to Indonesia, and three workers to Thailand. The Methodists have sent a missionary to Okinawa.

There is life and vigor among the Protestant Christians in the Philippines, even though they are a minority. A high degree of literacy is found among Christians; it is said that Evangelical Christians are 100 per cent literate. There is also an educated lay and ministerial leadership in the churches. It was in the Philippines that Dr. Frank Laubach first launched his adult literacy campaign, mostly among illiterate Muslims. The Protestant church in the Philippines is playing an important role, not only in the life of this land but also in the evangelization of East Asia.

CHARACTERISTICS OF EVANGELICAL CHRISTIANITY IN THE PHILIPPINES

Evangelical Christianity in the Philippines is American in expression. The Protestant workers who have entered the Philippines to proclaim the gospel and to organize Evangelical congregations have come predominantly from the United States. Their efforts have been supplemented by businessmen and government officials who take their religious faith seriously. These Christians have presented Christianity in the structural forms familiar in America. In organization, in worship, and in theological expression, the Filipino Protestant communities are carbon copies of their parent bodies in America.

In background, Evangelical Christianity in the Islands is Baptist-Congregational-Episcopal-Methodist-Presbyterian. Most of the American workers have been members of one of these five groups or of churches related to them. Filipino congregations reflect these denominational origins. Biblical literalism, millennialism, the social gospel, and other dominant American emphases are found scattered through the Islands. The Puritan attitude toward smoking, dancing, and the use of alcoholic beverages also is commonly found in the churches started by these missions. The crisis theology that has gained a foothold in Japan, Indonesia, and Ceylon is scarcely known; the writings of Barth and Brunner are not commonly read by the missionaries or Filipino Christians.

The Evangelical churches have not come to the Philippines to change practicing Roman Catholics into Protestants, but to lead sinners to repentance. Roman Catholicism has, however, created a predisposition to an acceptance of Protestantism. The large community of lapsed Roman Catholics and the great body of nominal Catholics who fail to find adequate religious certainty in the church of their parents have contributed to the rapid growth of the Evangelical churches.

RESOURCES OF FILIPINO EVANGELICALISM

The strength of Evangelical Christianity in the Philippines is shown in these ways:

1. The church is growing. Thus in the Filipino congregations, there is a buoyancy and hope that promote growth.

2. The membership is representative of most classes in the population. Thus, the church is a democratic rather than a class institution.

3. There is competent lay leadership to officiate in church services when ordained ministers are not available.

4. Most of the local congregations are self-supporting. (This, in some instances, involves part-time employment by ministers.) Foreign mission boards also continue to subsidize local churches in some lands. The Filipino churches still

accept grants from abroad for ecumenical work and the administration of such church organizations as the Federation of Christian Churches.

5. The educational level among ministers, due to the facilities for theological education, places the Filipino churches in a position to share some of their leadership with churches in other lands of Southeast Asia where the educational level is not equally high.

6. There is vitality in Filipino evangelicalism akin to New Testament certainty. This derives both from the emphasis upon revivalism and the desire to implement the Christian faith socially.

HANDICAPS IN THE EVANGELICAL MOVEMENT

On the other hand, serious obstacles to progress are evident.

1. There is too much dependence upon America. The Philippines are in Asia but not of it. Filipino acceptance of American support and guidance has prevented the Filipino Christian community from developing autonomy and self-support as fast as might otherwise have been possible.

2. The theology is neither fundamentalist nor liberal. A Filipino synthesis is needed.

3. There is strong Roman Catholic opposition. For the time being, the Evangelical churches enjoy a freedom supported by (a) the Constitution of the Republic of the Philippines, (b) free masonry, (c) strong anticlericalism among liberal Roman Catholics, and (d) American influence.

The Republic of the Philippines has granted religious freedom, a protection the national government has endeavored to guarantee. Provincial officials in numerous instances reflect Roman Catholic pressure. Protestant evangelists have been refused the right to preach. Protestants generally are fearful of a revived clericalism.

At a Manila conference on Christianity and Communism in February, 1951, several Filipino Christian leaders stated that Roman Catholicism was a greater menace to the Philippines than communism. No one present challenged them.

Former executive secretary of the Philippine Federation of Christian Churches, Juan Nabong, lists some of the causes of the growth of Protestantism in the Philippines:

Freedom of religion is guaranteed by our Constitution; no religious test is required for the exercise of civil or political rights; church properties used for religious purposes are tax exempt; no public money nor property is appropriated or used directly or indirectly for the use, benefit, or support of any church or denomination; only optional religious instruction is allowed in the public schools. With no material advantage given to any church by the government, Protestantism in the Philippines has run a race with others and has come out with flying colors at the close of the last fifty years. It is with pardonable pride and gratitude to God that we can now point to our innumerable churches in almost every town in the Philippines, our continuously increasing number of ministers and women workers, our Sunday schools, youth and women's societies, our schools and colleges, seminaries and Bible schools, our hospitals and schools of nursing, our dormitories and student centers, our radio stations, the translation and sale of the Bible in the different dialects, our literature production and distribution, and our monthly periodicals. Our record is so brilliant that he who wants may read it. In every international gathering, our delegates have discovered that the Philippines is one of the most successful mission fields in the world today.

CHAPTER 5

War and Communism

A group of influential Asians were entertaining a Westerner in a private home. The conversation turned to conditions in Southeast Asia.

"There is simply no way of estimating the harm done by war and communism," the most outspoken of the hosts said. "The war in the Pacific created havoc in the Philippines, Burma, and much of Malaya and Indonesia. There was physical destruction, yes, but there was also psychological damage. In the churches, as in local government, deep rifts still exist between those who consider themselves as having remained loyal and those accused of collaborating with the Japanese."

As for communism, he went on to say, "Here in our city you have seen how even some Christians have been deluded by the Reds. Keep your eyes and ears open in other places you visit. You will find some church members openly opposed to communism, some who defend it, and a much larger group unwilling or afraid to come out one way or the other. And of course the three groups distrust one another."

Every one of the lands of Southeast Asia knew the rule of Japanese forces during World War II. In some places the occupation was mild, in others brutal. In all, it was a bitter experience for the people. Some of the cities—notably Rangoon and Manila—were bombed by both Japanese and Allies. Church bodies suffered losses of buildings and personnel (losses that have not yet been completely made up). Some Christians were accused of collaborating with the enemy and were persecuted. The struggle for survival left little time for vigorous programs. Support from Western friends was cut off. Yet, despite all the hardships, in no region or country was the church obliterated during this trying period.

The Japanese surrender ended one difficult period and began another, that of reconstruction. Repairing the damages of occupation and overcoming the loss of leadership have been complicated in almost every land by continuing civil war or unrest. Still the churches are making a remarkable recovery, aided by foreign money and personnel. More church bodies exercise self-government than ever before. United church bodies dominate the scene in some of the lands. Yet it must be noted that, in a few areas, even where a united church exists, old denominational lines are reappearing, some new lines are being marked out, and small sects have multiplied.

Independence is confronting the churches of Southeast Asia with an awkward situation. Trained missionaries are available for help, but the churches aren't quite sure how to use them. The condition troubles Asian church leaders and is frustrating to some able missionaries.

WAR AND RECONSTRUCTION IN THAILAND

One aspect of the ordeal of war and reconstruction in Southeast Asia is reflected in the experience of the Christians of Thailand. Early in the war, the Buddhist-led government, a nominal ally of Japan, issued orders designed to secure religious uniformity. These were enforced more rigorously in rural areas than in the cities, where the officials, being closer to the Bangkok bureaucracy, were aware of the half-hearted purpose of the orders. Church members were herded by the police into temples and ordered to renounce their faith. Some Thai obeyed the order and renounced Christianity. Others dared to reply, "You can't do this to us. It is unconstitutional." A few even said, "We would be glad to die for Christ."

In the North, six families of new Christians were thrown into prison on charges that they intended to pray to the God of the Allies for victory. They were jailed for half a year. Imprisonment brought hunger, disease, and death to other Christians.

Such persecution cost the church heavily. Congregations were thinned by deaths and the number of people who recanted. In some churches, half of the congregations forsook Christianity.

On the other hand, the wartime demonstration of Christian courage has strengthened the morale of the churches and enhanced their reputation among Buddhists. The Thai people now know the power of the Christian faith in times of crisis, as well as its weakness. The churches and individual Christians defied the government by insisting upon civil rights at the time they were being denied.

A tower of strength among Thai Christians during the occupation was the man who is the present moderator of the Church of Christ in Thailand, the Reverend Puang Akkipin. Puang Akkipin has a convert's knowledge of the power of evangelism. As a young man, and a Buddhist, he stopped one day at a Christian street chapel in Bangkok. Casual conversation led to deep discussion, and eventually the witness of the mission's workers convinced him of his need of Christ. Despite his lack of education beyond grammar school level, he studied for the ministry under the guidance of an American missionary and became an ordained pastor.

Just before the war, he conducted a remarkable evangelistic campaign, traveling throughout Thailand by bicycle. And when Japanese power spread across his country, endangering and confusing the work of churches, Puang Akkipin provided pastoral guidance for many a leaderless Christian community. During the years of occupation, he initiated a "Weeks of Evangelism" campaign, visiting a village each week, holding three meetings daily.

The churches did not forget him. At the first meeting of the Church of Christ after the war ended, he was elected moderator. He has served since then, and the church bears the mark of his leadership. Under his guidance, an evangelism campaign was started that has almost doubled the membership of the churches. Thirty-nine new congregations have come to birth.

This ardent pastor, despite his limited training as a young man, has gathered a great fund of knowledge. His sermons are rich with quotations from his extremely wide reading; his leadership is the creation of a courageous and devoted spirit and an active and almost prophetic mind. His continued travels among the churches, now that he is moderator, are a source of strength and inspiration. One result has been the gathering of funds with which a four-story headquarters building was erected in Bangkok in 1954.

COMMUNISM IN INDOCHINA

Another example of the effects of war on the churches can be taken from Indochina. This country fell early and easily to the Japanese. Occupation meant much the same as it did in Thailand: a government subservient to the Japanese; Christians trying to be true to their faith under hard circumstances. But there was one radically different factor in Indochina, the Viet Minh.

Viet Minh is an abbreviation of a long native name that, translated, means the League for the Independence of Viet Nam. It was organized in late 1941 by Ho Chi-minh, a fanatical nationalist and friend of the Soviet Union. Ho had spent most of his life either underground in Indochina or in China and Russia, agitating for the freedom of his native land from French colonialism.

The strength developed by the Viet Minh was derived from the mistakes of the French. France's colonial policy in Indochina had many flaws. Resentment against them was intensified by a postwar Allied occupation that paid little heed to the restlessness of the people under foreign domination. The flames of feeling were taken advantage of by the opportunistic Communists, who exploit all human need and make capital of other nations' mistakes.

The long war between France and the Viet Minh began with the French attack on Hanoi in December, 1946, and

was brought to an uneasy truce in 1954 with the establishment of the artificial boundary that cut Viet Nam in half
near the seventeenth parallel of latitude and changed it into
two hostile states.

Ho Chi-minh and his advisers are Communists. Most of
the villagers who have stood behind them only want their
freedom. Non-Communists themselves, these villagers accepted the leadership of the one group they felt could
wrest control from the hands of the French. Some Roman
Catholic youths in Hanoi were asked how they could work
for Ho.

"We must be free," one of them replied. "Only by revolution can we gain independence. Only Ho Chi-minh can
lead the revolution."

FACTORS THAT ENCOURAGE COMMUNISM

Communism has developed more fully in Indochina than
elsewhere in Southeast Asia. Yet the churches in the other
lands of the area must reckon with its power. Reds directed
Huk outbreaks in the Philippines. Five thousand Communists in Malaya's jungles have hampered the development of that rich land. The Communist Party is alive and
virulent in Indonesia and Burma. It is Christianity's adver-
sary everywhere.

Violent changes in the economies of Southeast Asia have
resulted in poverty and distress. Though the entire area is
rich in resources—among them oil, tin, tea, and rubber—
nature's wealth has not been developed for the benefit of
the people, either under the pre-Western native rulers or by
the Western colonists. Deaths from malnutrition occur in
the midst of plenty. Inflation and soaring costs of food add

to the suffering. Such conditions afford fertile soil for the sowing of Communist seed, and communism plays up inequalities against the background of its own tempting picture of a proletarian paradise.

A Communist agent professes his party's interest in the downtrodden. Many a naïve person inclined toward Christianity is apt to swallow the party line because of its similarity to the Hebrew prophets' demands for social justice. This is likely to be true particularly in Asia.

Before the Reds took control of China, an American was visiting that country. Twenty years before, he had been a social-evangelistic missionary in a distant Chinese city. His return to China brought him to Chungking, where he was stealthily approached by a stranger.

"Do you remember Mr. X?" he was asked.

Yes, the American did remember. His mind recalled a highly intelligent, fairly rich member of the gentry class who, in far distant Fukien Province, had experienced a striking conversion and had become very active in church work. As time passed, however, Mr. X had felt frustrated by his country's slowness in reform. Finally he had left his home and family to enroll as a Communist Party worker.

The messenger went on, "Would you care to see Mr. X? He wants to talk with you, but he can not enter the city openly. His life is in danger."

The meeting was arranged. Mr. X explained that the Old Testament prophetic messages had seemed to him to culminate in communism's program; Christianity was too slow. He told a story of Communist activity, of growing doubt, disillusionment, and frustration.

Then he summed up, "Teacher, both sides of my country's leadership are corrupt and brutal. I have turned away from communism, and my life is forfeit to that side. I am wanted by the secret police and would be killed by them. I was convinced of the ineffectiveness of Christianity, and I turned away from it. Now I have entered a Buddhist monastery as a novice. Perhaps if I turn from all human activity I can find peace. This is good-by."

Without any question, the churches of Southeast Asia must face the challenge of communism, both as an open antagonist and as a subtle, infiltrating agent. There is equally no doubt that they are facing it with intelligence and with devotion to Christ.

This chapter has dealt with the effects of war and communism over a large area. The great Malay Peninsula is a part of that area, and its story tells what war and communism can do to one land and its people.

CHAPTER 6

Malaya

A widely traveled American returned from a visit to the Malay Peninsula and said, "I never saw anything like it in any other area. It is a tightly held colony, yet the ruling government is committed to grant early freedom from colonial rule. People of alien blood in the population outnumber the indigenous race. In Singapore, I saw an English-speaking church in which there were at least a dozen nations represented and three color strains—yet most of the other churches are organized into language groups. What a land!"

His picture was not overdrawn. Look at some of the facts. More than six million people inhabit British Malaya, an area composed of the Federation of Malaya and the crown colony of Singapore. The Federation includes the four former Federated Malay States, the five former Unfederated States, and the British settlements of Malacca and Penang. Singapore has as dependencies Christmas Island and the Cocos Islands.

The Malays who comprise three sevenths of the population are closely related to the peoples of Indonesia. They are Muslims by religion, closely knit in village, and engaged primarily in agriculture. Almost an equal number are Chinese, concentrated in the cities or employed in tin mines and on rubber plantations. Almost three quarters of a million Indians and a few thousand Westerners, living primarily in the port cities, make up the remainder.

Malaya is one of the few remaining places in Asia where the British still exercise a degree of governmental power. For some years, it has been the scene of a bloody struggle between Communist guerrillas and British forces, a war costly for both sides. The Communists contend they are fighting for the independence of the peninsula. Great Britain refuses to grant independence under circumstances that would assure Communist domination.

The Chinese resent the restriction of certain political privileges to the Malay people; the Malays resent the economic prosperity and commercial monopoly exercised by the Chinese; the Indians are fearful of being squeezed between the two dominant races.

HISTORY

Since a written language has been a late development, the history of the area is not so full nor so clear-cut as would be desirable. It is known, however, that as early as the second century Indian traders were frequent visitors, and it is almost certain that settlements of Indians were established. Somewhere about the twelfth century, Arab and Persian traders began to come to Malaysia, as the Malay Peninsula and nearby islands came to be known. Singapore may have been a port as early as the twelfth century, although Marco Polo does not mention it.

The spices from the Orient had become so essential in Europe that Western nations sought new sea routes to the Orient. The Portuguese rounded Africa and in 1511 arrived at Malacca, which they captured and made into a strongly fortified walled city. Francis Xavier established a mission in the city and from it traveled to other parts of Malaya, visiting Singapore in 1552.

The Portuguese, once they had charted a course around the Cape of Good Hope, established three settlements en route to the Spice Islands in addition to the one at Malacca. The Dutch dislodged the Portuguese in 1641, and they in turn were replaced by the British after 1795, except for a brief interval, 1818-24. The Japanese were the latest of the occupying powers, sweeping down the Malay Peninsula by land, instead of coming by sea as expected, and finally capturing Singapore on February 12, 1942. They held control until after their defeat in the summer of 1945.

During the early centuries of its history, Malaya was not a unified country in the ordinary sense of the word. The Malays and the increasing number of Indian and Chinese immigrant settlers were all under the rule of chieftains or sultans who were frequently at war with one another.

THE PEOPLE OF MALAYA

Representatives of many of the groups to be found in this land of intricately mingled races may be seen at the services in English held at Wesley Church in Singapore. A minister who preached at a recent vesper service was told that not only was his sermon reaching uncounted individuals of many groups through a radio broadcast, but at least ten nationalities were represented in the congregation.

There were Chinese of four dialect groups, Indians of two, and Burmans. There were Singhalese, Thai, and Bataks. There were Americans, Englishmen, Irishmen, Germans, and Scandinavians.

Some of the world's most primitive peoples are found in the interior of the peninsula. The Semang are Negritos, small and dark with curly hair, and they are hunters rather than farmers. The Sakai plant rice and tapioca and manufacture cooking vessels and clothing, but otherwise they live by hunting and fishing. In appearance they resemble the Malays, and in part of the peninsula the two groups intermingle.

Beginning with the Japanese occupation, a renaissance began among the Malay people that has transformed their quiet, easy-going ways, making them alert and aggressive. Methodist missionary R. A. Blasdell points to a growing political consciousness, the realization of weakness growing out of their economic position and their inability to compete with the Chinese in business. *Merdeka* (freedom), the word that unified their Indonesian cousins against the Dutch, became their slogan, too.

The United Malay National Organization, one of the two leading political parties, under the influence of Dato Onn Bin Ja'afar, was established to protect the rights of the Malays within the new Federation of Malaya. Despite the privileged economic situation of the Chinese, the Malays were determined to be the dominant political group in the nation.

In an attempt to overcome the disparity between the economic position of Malays and Chinese, Malay leaders are exhorting their people to enter business and industry, to cultivate a variety of crops, to work hard, to train the Malay children, and to prepare for leadership. Malay population growth is behind that of the Chinese because of high infant mortality, which in turn is attributable in part to Malay customs and fatalism, as well as to inadequate medical facilities in the villages.

Chinese are concentrated in the cities. In Singapore, they now constitute 85 per cent of the population and control the economic life, though Indian, Ceylonese, and British interests are also in evidence. Chinese are discriminated against in government by a British policy that reserves civil posts for Malays. As the Malays are lacking in education, this means a slow devolution from British control. This has caused some Chinese to be unenthusiastic about independence, fearing that restrictions similar to those that have been imposed in Thailand may be extended to Malaya. They have also been afraid of the development of a Pan-Malay movement that would merge Malaya with Indonesia.

However, a realistic appraisal of the national situation by both Malays and Chinese has caused them to recognize the advantages of working together for the best interests of all. The Malayan Chinese Association, representing the more than two million Chinese, was organized to maintain proper relations between the Malay and Chinese communities and to support the government law-and-order campaign in the face of Communist terror, as well as to protect the rights of the Chinese. In 1955, the Association formed a political alliance with the United Malay National Organization; both groups are aware that independence would not be workable without cooperation between their communities.

The Chinese and Malays are united in wanting to break the monopoly of colonial control of government positions.

They plan gradually to take over government posts so that when independence comes the transfer of authority will involve only the top positions, a procedure that the United States demonstrated effectively in the Philippine Islands. If this plan succeeds in Malaya, it will indicate to Asia that a reasonable revolution without an explosion is feasible.

The extension of citizenship to persons of non-Malay ancestry has provided the opportunity of integrating Chinese youth into the total life of the area. Pro-Peking sympathies are on the wane.

The Indians, sympathizing with neither of the two dominant groups, hope for continued British rule.

The Communist Party was constitutional until 1948, when the Reds' resort to violence led to their being forced underground. The party was and is composed principally of remnants of the British-armed Chinese Liberation Army that harassed the Japanese. Today it is a force of five thousand guerrillas who have their own political and military organization, which exacts taxes and information from the villages and makes war against soldiers, police, planters, and informers. Civilians on peaceable errands and foreign missionaries enter the areas without harm. Every month a hundred or more "bandits" and thirty to forty police, soldiers, and civilians are killed in the skirmishes. Europeans on the rubber estates are under constant threat and thus must travel in armored cars.

Because the scattered groups of Chinese squatters at the jungle's edge had been the eyes and ears of the Communists, 500,000 of them are being resettled in communities called new villages. New houses have been built for them in enclosed, guarded villages. No one may leave a village after sundown, and a twenty-three-hour-a-day ban on travel is imposed if there is suspicion of cooperation by the villagers with the guerrilla forces. The government is also seeking to starve out the Communists by food control. The amount of food permitted in a given area is controlled, so that it cannot be shared with the guerrillas.

Malaya has been called a melting pot of many races. But as has been shown, the melting pot has not yet melted the races into one nation. Each of the different communal and racial groups exists as a separate entity in the life of the country.

This exclusive spirit has invaded the church as well, though of late some interracial congregations have come into existence. On the whole, the Chinese and Indian congregations exist as separate units; in the Methodist Church with American connection, the Chinese Conference functions separately. The Ceylon Tamil and the Indian Tamil Christians do not mix freely, and this unfortunate cleavage among the Tamil Christians runs right through the peninsula.

PREWAR CHURCH HISTORY

The Christian gospel was brought first to Malaya by Francis Xavier in 1545. His body was buried at Malacca until its removal to Goa, a small settlement in India under control of Portugal. The Roman Church today numbers 93,000, as compared with the Protestant community of 80,000.

Largest of the Protestant church bodies is the Methodist, which has developed from American missionary activities. Beginning in 1885, Methodists extended their operations from Malaya to the Philippines, British North Borneo, and Indonesia, all of these now separate units. Today the Methodist Church in Malaya has approximately 15,500 communicant members, the nucleus of an estimated Methodist community of 29,000. One half of the Methodists are concentrated in Singapore. One third of the two hundred members of the staff also are working in Singapore, two thirds in the Federation of Malaya. One third of the sixty-nine ordained Asian ministers on the staff are Tamils. The other forty-six are Chinese, who speak both Straits-Chinese and vernacular Chinese dialects.

Tracey K. Jones, former minister of Wesley Church in Singapore, states that the church is growing faster today than ever before, for it is now popular to be a Christian. The hold of Buddhism on the Chinese is relaxing as they look less and less to China as the home country.

There are two Presbyterian church bodies in Malaya. One, with about three thousand members, is the Chinese Christian Church of Malaya. Though developed entirely in Malaya from British Presbyterian activities among Chinese after 1856, it was regarded as an extension of mission work begun in Hokkien and Swatow about 1848. From 1948 to 1954, this body was affiliated as the Malay Synod of the Church of Christ in China.

Malacca was among the first mission stations occupied by Protestant missionaries. Dr. William Milne of the London Missionary Society, with the assistance of Dr. Robert Morrison of China, began work here in 1814. Dr. Milne had burned with desire to serve in China, but the Chinese at that time refused to permit Christian missionaries in their land, so he served for a time in Malaya. He founded the first Anglo-Chinese college and established a printing press on which he published Dr. Morrison's Chinese translation of the New Testament.

Dr. James Legge, whose history-making English translation of the Chinese classics is a monument to him, served as principal of the Anglo-Chinese College at Malacca for three years after 1840. Following the defeat of China by the British in a brief war, the peace treaty opened five China ports to missionaries. All save one of the LMS missionaries departed for the North. The Reverend B. P. Keasburry then became the sole Protestant missionary in Singapore. He supported himself by operating the printing press and by teaching. He organized the first congregation of the English Presbyterian Mission, translated the Bible into Malay, and wrote hymns and tracts in Malay. He died while preaching in the Malay Chapel, with these words on his lips: "A time is coming when the Mohammedans will acknowledge and worship the Saviour."

Prior to the Japanese occupation, only two Presbyterian missionary families remained in Malaya. Today many ex-China workers are attached to the Chinese Christian Church of Malaya: English, Irish, and Scottish Presbyterians, and missionaries of the London Missionary Society. In a number of Chinese-speaking churches, services in English are now being conducted for the younger Chinese and for Europeans on the foreign-owned plantations.

The Anglican Church is a century old. The Church of England, Diocese of Singapore, has close to six thousand communicants. The Anglican community numbers more than 16,000. The church first worked in Malaya among the British settlers. After the Society for the Propagation of the

Gospel entered Malaya in 1848, work was begun among the Tamils, the Singhalese, and the Chinese. An Anglican chaplain started the first school in Penang in 1816, which may well have been the first English school in Southeast Asia. The Church of England Zenana Mission first started a school for girls in Malaya.

THE POSTWAR CHURCH

The Japanese occupation marked a real change in Malayan church life. Prior to 1941, there had been little interdenominational fellowship. The fall of Singapore forced cooperation among Christians. The work of Anglican Bishop John Leonard Wilson on behalf of Asian church members, after other missionaries had been interned, stimulated unity and interchurch cooperation. Conversations during these days led to the establishment of Trinity College for the training of Anglican, Presbyterian, and Methodist ministers, offering instruction both in English and Chinese. The termination of foreign aid forced the churches to accept the responsibility for church operations and support.

The Methodist Church of Malaya through its Board of Home Missions has sent three native workers to Sarawak, Borneo, as missionaries to the Dyak people.

There are many groups that have entered or expanded their operations after the closing of the missionary door in China. Some of these cooperate with the Malaya Christian Council. There are four Indian Churches. Two of them are affiliated with the Mar Thoma Syrian Church of Malabar, South India; their membership is about five hundred. The two Tamil Evangelical Lutheran Churches have a membership of somewhat more than five hundred.

The Plymouth Brethren (two thousand), Seventh-Day Adventists (twelve thousand), the Assemblies of God, the Christian and Missionary Alliance, Christian Missions in Many Lands (nearly two thousand), and the Southern Baptist Convention present the peoples of Malaya with the varied character of Protestantism. The Overseas Missionary Fellowship (China Inland Mission) has transferred approximately fifty of its China staff to Malaya.

These accessions from China have expanded the Christian operations, but they have also increased denominational rivalry and have resulted in criticism and recrimination by those who feel that they alone have the truth. Yet, the Reverend Wallace Merwin, a secretary of the Division of Foreign Missions of the National Council of the Churches of Christ in the U.S.A., following a visit to Malaya in 1953, said that there is a fine spirit of cooperation, especially as demonstrated by the Methodists, the largest church.

CHARACTERISTICS OF THE CHURCH

A strange characteristic of the church in Malaya is that it exists in its entirety among the immigrant population, namely, the Chinese and the Indians, and not at all among the Malays, the native inhabitants. Christian Malays may be numbered on the fingers of two hands! Since the Treaty of Pangkor in 1874, Britain has recognized that the official religion of the Malay States is Islam. It has long been held that any attempt by Christians to convert Muslim Malays would be a breach of the spirit of this treaty.

When, in 1950 at Penang, two Muslims were converted to Christianity, it almost led to a riot. The police intervened and spirited away the two converts. However, the Methodist

Church maintains Christian hostels in Malacca for Malay boys and girls.

Another feature of the Christian enterprise in the Federation of Malaya and Singapore is that it specializes in educational work more than in any other. In Malaya, as elsewhere in East Asia, Christian missions have been the pioneers in the field of education. Today, out of the ninety-seven aided English schools on the peninsula, more than one half are operated by Christian missions. Sixty per cent of the English education for girls is under Christian auspices.

Instruction in the sixty-three Methodist church schools is all in English. Seven of them have missionary principals; fifty-six are headed by Chinese. A total of 42,000 students are enrolled. Although these schools are openly Christian, the government pays the salary of all staff members, determines the curriculum, and matches the church-contributed dollars in erecting buildings, which are then owned by the church. There is complete freedom of religious instruction; Bible study is a part of the curriculum and Cambridge examinations are permitted in Bible subjects.

An even finer feature of the church is its group of Christian men and women. Among them are leaders in the field of church-sponsored schools: principals, headmasters, even country-wide secretaries of education. Several have been honored by the Queen. Strong preachers, both Indian and Chinese, minister to large self-supporting churches, many of which contribute liberally to home and foreign missionary projects.

To point up the influence of Christians in the area, let us introduce Chen Su-lan, M.D., now retired. Born in Foochow, China, and for a time a student in the Christian schools of that city, he early emigrated to Singapore, where for decades he has been active in the Foochow-speaking Methodist church. We cite some of his activities, outside his local congregational service: (1) He led in the Anti-Social-Vice Campaign that was responsible for the abolition of state-regulated brothels in Malaya in 1928-29. (2) According to a number of informants, he was also responsible, almost single-handedly at first, for agitation against government licensing of opium. The agitation led to the League of Nations Enquiry Commission's coming to Malaya to study the situation. Recognition of opium-smoking as a vice and plans for the abolition of the opium dens followed, despite the immense revenue derived by government (reportedly 20 million Straits dollars in 1941). During his leadership in this campaign, Chen received threats of personal violence and even of official banishment. (3) He founded and operated the Singapore Anti-Opium Clinic that treated and helped cure more than seven thousand addicts. (4) He was the spark plug for the early anti-tuberculosis campaigns. The Rotary Club backed this effort by one of its members and this, in turn, led to the establishment of the Singapore Anti-TB Clinic. (5) He was one of the founders of the Chinese Y.M.C.A. in Singapore and has twice served as its president.

If, as has been said, "the best proof of Christianity is a Christian," here is one man who gives evidence among the many outstanding Indian and Chinese churchmen of Malaya.

NATIONALISM IN MALAYA

The mood of the Malays has altered because of and since the war. The spirit of nationalism is growing among them, a fact that most likely will compound the difficulties of mission operations in Malay villages if governmental permission is granted. New opportunities for Christian activity have developed. The Malays want increased and enlarged educational facilities. Christian educational advisers would be welcomed by the Malay community, especially if they should establish a system comparable to that which the Chinese community enjoys. The Malays know they must improve their agriculture. They would welcome agricultural technicians to supplement governmental assistance, particularly if the specialists entered into intimate contact with the people.

Malay leaders are aware of the social evils produced by urbanization and Westernization of life, concerning which their own religious tradition and writings are silent. Christian social workers approaching the Malay communities sympathetically could alleviate these social evils and the inequalities. This openness constitutes an opportunity in which the Christian church may share. The Malays have been responsive to Christian literacy efforts. They probably would accept other Christian assistance if tendered sympathetically.

Quite a number of the city churches in Singapore and the Federation of Malaya have been experimenting with part-time ministers. Most of these are employed in Christian schools but are also pastors of congregations. This enables the churches to have an educated ministry without the complete burden of its support resting on the congregations.

It may not be unfair to remark that one notices in Malaya and Singapore a colonial atmosphere in which the leadership of the churches tends to be non-Asian. There may also be a conscious or unconscious reflection of the political atmosphere in the life of the churches. Sometimes this may arise from Asian opinion, which prefers a "neutral" foreigner to a national who belongs to one group or another within the church.

Immediately after the last war, the Malaya Christian Council came into existence with headquarters at Singapore and regional councils at Penang, Ipoh, and Kuala Lumpur. It has been greatly strengthened by the recent appointment of a full-time secretary. Under the auspices of this Council a vigorous evangelistic drive is under way in the new villages of the Federation. There are now over a hundred resident workers, Chinese and foreign missionaries belonging to different denominations, as well as over 150 voluntary workers, whose itinerary extends to approximately a hundred new villages. Students of Trinity College took part in this work during the 1953 summer vacation.

Two vans equipped with movie and projection equipment are now touring these villages. This development represents a new outreach of the churches in the last two years; it also means that thousands of Chinese and Indians are for the first time coming into touch with the Christian gospel and witness. An interesting aspect of the development of new village communities is that a number of ex-China missionaries are now associated with the undertaking, not as missionaries but as government officers in resettlement, administration, education, etc. This really means a secular missionary effort in relation to the Christian movement in the East, since definitely Christian attitudes are brought to bear upon the problems of local government.

The Federation and Singapore are among the few areas of East Asia that are still under colonial rule. The cry for political independence is not, however, as audible in Malaya as it is in other parts of Asia still under foreign domination. This may be due partly to the communal jealousy that has existed between the Malays and the Chinese, who are about equal in number. The new political alignment between the groups should effect a significant change.

How to weld the Malays, Chinese, and Indians into one strong nation, able to take over the reins of the government when Malaya becomes independent, is one of the most difficult problems for Britain to tackle. It will be interesting to watch the British attempt to steer the ship of state into calm waters and complete the unification of the crew, before they hand over the captaincy to a new skipper. But if the church can exemplify in its own life the spirit in which racial tensions can be overcome and show how its fellowship transcends the barriers of race, it will set a true course for the state.

CHAPTER 7

The Religious Climate

Three men who lived hundreds of years ago are partly responsible for the differences that exist between Southeast Asians and Americans. Their lives and teachings are the foundations of three great religions whose marks are plain on the face of Asia. Yet these religions have scarcely any effect on the lives of Americans.

The men were Mohammed, Gautama, and Confucius. The faiths founded upon them are Islam, Buddhism, and Confucianism. These three, with Hinduism, claim the loyalty of the vast majority of the people of Southeast Asia and mold the cultures in which Evangelical Christians live and work.

Adherents of Islam and Buddhism outnumber all the others. Indonesia is one of the larger nations professing Islam. The Malays of the Malay Peninsula and the Moros of the Philippines also revere Mohammed. The Burmese, the Thai people, and the Cambodians are Buddhist. Their Buddhism is the Hinayana form, orthodox and conservative. It is found also in Ceylon. Confucianism exists wherever Chinese are concentrated. Hinduism is the religion of the Balinese.

These ancient non-Christian faiths have recently become resurgent and aggressive, and, in places, are in open conflict with Christianity.

ISLAM

Islam is built upon the teaching of Mohammed, who lived about six centuries after Christ. Born in Mecca and orphaned early, he grew up in the care of relatives. As a child and as a youth, he traveled by caravan to Syria and other lands. When he was twenty-five, he entered the service of a wealthy widow whom he eventually married. Her wealth gave him leisure that enabled him to exercise his already strong bent toward introspection and the search for religious truth. Gradually he came to the conviction that God was calling him as a prophet; the first converts to the new faith he founded were his wife, his adopted children, and close friends.

Mohammed conceived his mission as being to proclaim Allah as the one God. He moved through a stormy career, gathering converts and making enemies. After the death of his first wife, he taught polygamy, and himself, reputedly, had eleven wives. Before his death in A.D. 632 he was master of all Arabia and some of his armed forces had penetrated other lands.

What of his teachings? The sacred book of Islam, named the Koran, contains many of these; some seem to a Christian to be unworthy of notice, some of lofty purpose, some mediocre. Every Muslim must hold to six fundamental articles of faith:

The oneness of God. This is central in all of Mohammed's teaching and is the one part of the creed repeated daily by all Muslims: "There is no god but Allah, and Mohammed is the apostle of Allah."

The prophets. Muslims recognize many prophets, including Adam, Abraham, Noah, and Moses from the Hebrew religion, and Jesus as the "sinless Prophet." But they claim that the prophetic line reached its peak in Mohammed.

Sacred books. Islam recognizes many of these, including Hebrew and Christian writings, but "the" book is the Koran.

Angels. Although this religion worships only one God, a large place is made for angels.

The day of judgment, when the evil deeds of an individual are weighed against the good.

Predestination, which means that everything that happens is foreordained by Allah.

Muslims are among the most faithful religionists in all the world. Their strongly held faith is dominant in parts of Southeast Asia and formidable in others. In Malaya, it makes Christian work among the Malays all but impossible. The British early agreed that Islam would be the official religion of the Malay states. Thus attempts to convert Muslims to Christianity contradicted the spirit of this agreement, and while there are occasional converts from Islam, they are few indeed. There are Muslims in parts of the Philippine Islands, particularly the Moros, who show deep devotion to their faith.

Probably Islam is more widely practiced in Indonesia than in any of the other countries of Southeast Asia. This is due to the early and active missionary work done by Muslim traders long before the arrival of the Dutch. Islam had all but conquered Java by that time and, in order to prevent friction, Dutch officials refused to admit Christian evangelists to the island until 1851. At one time the Dutch impounded a Japanese translation of the New Testament, at another they kept a convert waiting five years to be baptized.

It is worthy of emphasis, however, that despite the smallness of the Christian communities on Java, the 85,000 members form the largest Christian church in the Muslim world.

BUDDHISM

As in the case of Islam, Buddhism is based upon the life of a man, Gautama by name, and upon his teaching as enlarged upon by his disciples. Gautama Buddha (Buddha means "the enlightened") was born into a wealthy family with aristocratic and warrior traditions. Most authorities agree that he was born about 560 B.C., in northern India. At the age of thirty, just after the birth of his son, he renounced his family and the comforts of his position and set out to find salvation.

He searched for several years, and at last enlightenment came to him as he sat meditating beneath a bo tree. Slowly, he acquired what he believed to be true knowledge. He became the Buddha, and in the twenty-five centuries that have elapsed since his experience, millions have followed him.

In briefest compass, Buddhism offers four "Noble Truths" that are basic:

Existence involves suffering.

Suffering is caused by desire.

To escape suffering, one must get rid of desire.

To be free from desire, one must follow certain rules of right living.

The history of the spread of Buddhism over India, across Burma and Tibet to the northern and eastern reaches of the Asian continent, even to the islands of Japan, can only be mentioned here. Buddhism has suffered a long decline, particularly in India, where it gave way to Hinduism. In many other countries of Asia, however, it can be found in its two forms, the Mahayana and the Hinayana.

Today Buddhism is enjoying a revival. This is evident in Burma, for example, where the Burmese are almost solidly Buddhist and where visitors in the southern part of the country are invariably impressed by the streams of saffron-robed priests daily going about their tasks. In Thailand, too, and in parts of Indochina, Buddhism is a strong religious force, while among the Chinese population of the different countries of Southeast Asia are to be found many Buddhist temples and priests.

CONFUCIANISM

These Chinese folk in foreign lands are also the people among whom Confucianism has its supreme influence. Its impact on the religious climate of Southeast Asia is relatively weak.

Kung-fu-tse, or Confucius, as he has come to be most widely known, was a Chinese philosopher who lived in the sixth century B.C. The youngest of eleven children, he lived in poverty during his youth. In his mature years, he held government positions, but he was best known as a teacher. His influence was immense; three thousand disciples were said to have followed him at one time. Teacher, government official, adviser to rulers of the early Chinese states, and in his old age an author and the compiler of the ancient teachings on which he based so much of his own system of philosophy and ethics—this was Confucius.

Confucianism cannot be described as briefly as Islam and Buddhism. With a dim, somewhat skeptical view of the supernatural but deep reverence for ancestors, most of the teachings of the sage have practical application to the everyday lives of men and women. These characteristics lead some authorities to label Confucianism as a system of ethics and not a religion in the true sense.

The ethical teachings, concisely stated, are: that human nature is good and that evil is unnatural; that the human will is completely free and men are their own masters; that a person is good not for future reward but for the very sake of being good; and that a person cannot look for help from outside sources, such as gods or other supernatural influences. The ideal Confucius set up was to be a "superior man," meaning to be the best possible under one's circumstances, to follow the "middle way" and not to go to extremes, and to observe loyally the five relations—of subject and ruler, of son and father, of husband and wife, of elder and younger brother, and of friend and friend.

HINDUISM

Hinduism, like Confucianism, is limited in its influence in Southeast Asia. It is found primarily among people who have migrated from India, particularly those living in Burma, Thailand, and Indonesia.

No single man is behind Hinduism. Its origins are buried in the forgotten days when men did not know how to write down what they knew or thought. Hinduism is extremely difficult to define, because it means different things to different Hindus. It has certain characteristics today; one of the most familiar is the idea of the transmigration of souls. This belief holds that when a person dies he is reborn in a higher or lower level of animal existence, depending upon the good or evil he did in the life just ended. The law of Karma—that one reaps what one sows—embodies the belief. To the Hindu, Karma binds men to the wheel of life. The goal of religion is to escape that relentless wheel and "find ultimate release from the ceaseless round of life." Hinduism emphasizes not the present world but the world to come.

The priestly class of Hindus, the Brahmans, are powerful in the extreme. They are at the top of the caste system that plays so important a part in Hindu thought and practice.

Temples of Hinduism are found throughout Southeast Asia; Hindu priests, holy days, and festival parades add distinctive colors to the tapestry of life. However, the total Indian population in the area is small. Something over half a million Indians each in Burma and in Malaya, including Singapore, form the two large communities. In the other areas, the numbers range from a thousand-plus in the Philippines up to some 27,000 in Indonesia.

NATIONALISM VERSUS CHRISTIANITY

No report on the non-Christian religions would be complete without mentioning nationalism. In recent years, love of country in Southeast Asia has become more than is implied in the dictionary's definition of patriotism. The nationalism of today approaches fanatic religion in the heat of its zeal and the strength of its emotionalism. It has been a rallying point, making possible the 1955 Bandung Conference of representatives from Asian and African nations. Southeast Asia's politicians, seeking to awake their supporters, are not averse to reviving old religions to unite their countries. In such an atmosphere, the average citizen is likely to confuse temples and capitols.

There is another side to this coin. For while many non-Christian faiths may be called in support of nationalism, and vice versa, Christianity is handicapped by its history of having gone hand in hand with colonialism. Non-Christian Asians regard the Christian religion as an appendage of Western colonialism and civilization. They have regarded their Christian neighbors with suspicion, and point to what has happened in certain areas. For example, the Moluccas, which are the home of a substantial number of Protestants, rebelled against the new state of Indonesia. When Burma divorced itself from the British Commonwealth, many leaders of the Karen revolt against the Burman Government were Christians. The hesitation of some of the Asian churches to readmit missionaries does not reflect Christian wishes, but is designed to disabuse non-Christian neighbors of suspicions that Christians are tools of the colonial powers.

The handicaps under which Dutch missionaries in Indonesia and American missionaries in Burma operate are extreme. Chinese church bodies in Indonesia were unable to invite American personnel after China entered the Korean War, so high did anti-American feelings run within Chinese communities. Christian communities are parts of national communities and are limited in their outreach by the attitudes and prevailing practices of the society of which they are a part.

Even governments, in some instances, are seeking to limit

missionaries to humanitarian services, such as educational and medical work. They claim that the preaching of the gospel must be left to the nationals or must be omitted entirely. Missionaries are excluded now from the Viet Minh area of Indochina. No evangelistic work is permitted by the British on the Malay Peninsula. The Burman Government limits the number and functions of American missionaries.

The missionary enterprise of the nineteenth century led Eastern peoples to identify Christianity with Western culture, institutions, and customs. (The same is true of the mission work of some sects today.) Non-Christian religions and cultures were to be uprooted and destroyed if Asians were to be saved. Twentieth century missionaries with a liberal theology tended to go easier on non-Christian faiths and cultures, to the extent of making Christianity their crown and fulfillment. Another attitude was that the Christian faith was independent of culture—that a people could be Christianized without affecting their day-to-day living. The main stream of the Christian church holds that Christianity is the unique revelation of God.

Every one of these views of Christianity implies that it is superior. Non-Christians resent the implication and resist the religion. To this hostility is added the fact that Christian churches are aliens in some parts of the world. Furthermore, Western workers too commonly have an attitude of superiority.

While most educated Asians admire the character and goodness of Christ, they do not accept the Christ as Saviour or join the fellowship of those who call themselves Christian. To the ancient world, the offense of Christianity was the

Cross; today in East Asia, the offense is the church. And yet Christianity attracts Asian peoples. They see it bringing something new and valuable, new ideals and personalities, selfless service. Some of them, aware that the older religions are inadequate for the needs of the new day, wonder if Christianity may not point the way to a solution of their problems.

CHAPTER 8

The Church in the Land of Pagodas

Romanticized by Kipling, occupied by the Japanese, liberated by the Allies, repossessed by the Burmans [1] in 1948, and devastated in civil war since that time, Burma struggles toward national unity and political maturity. In such a land, the Christian church lives and grows.

A GLANCE AT BURMA'S HISTORY

The Burmese, for all their preaching of peace, have been nurtured for centuries on war. Pulitzer prize winner James A. Michener writes, "For nearly a thousand years, Burman warriors have been going forth to sack Southwest Asia or fleeing homeward to await the shock of invasion. The Burmans have been extraordinarily brave, conspicuously nationalistic, and willing to wage war against any enemy, or among themselves if no aliens were available." [2]

[1] We have adopted for this book the distinction employed by Lawrence K. Rosinger in *The State of Asia*. A "Burman" is a citizen of Burma; a "Burmese" is a member of the dominant linguistic and cultural group.

[2] *The Voice of Asia*, by James A. Michener, p. 213. New York, Random House, 1951. Used by permission.

These Asian forays and wars were climaxed in the nineteenth century when Great Britain and Burma opened hostilities. The latter had been under British influence through the East India Company since about 1612. It was annexed in 1885 and administered as a part of British India, but was separated from Indian administration in 1937. The Japanese invaded the land in 1941 and soon occupied practically all of its territory. Post-retreat Allied bombings of Japanese installations destroyed two thirds of Burma's production facilities, damaged communications, and wrecked such cities as had not been destroyed on the eve of retreat.

Britain's postwar plans were to retain Burma as a dominion within the empire. Nationalistic developments rendered this policy untenable. Constituent Assembly elections in April, 1947, gave 90 per cent of the seats to the Anti-Fascist People's Freedom League. Following the election, the Prime Minister and the Assembly announced that Burma would dissolve its Empire relations and establish the autonomous Union of Burma.

In July, seven of the Executive Council members, including the prime minister himself, Aung San, were assassinated. In October, the new prime minister, Thakin Nu (now called U Nu) and British Prime Minister Clement Attlee signed an agreement constituting Burma as independent and sovereign. The establishment took place on January 4, 1948, and on April 19, Burma became a member of the United Nations. The constitution is a synthesis of Western liberalism and Marxism.

Hardly had the sovereign nation been established when within Burma armed bands and numerous political parties began to attack it. After a Communist conference held in

Calcutta, India, in February, 1948, strikes and an army mutiny occurred.

In September, the Karens in the army demonstrated their strong position. By March, 1949, the government was virtually a prisoner in Rangoon and considered going underground. For one year, its position was tenuous, but then its policy of playing one faction against the other reduced the number of its enemies. Since 1950, the government increasingly has had a stronger control on the life of the nation, incidents have decreased, and efforts are being made to implement adopted policies.

SOCIAL LIFE

The Burmese people are individualistic and democratic. The distribution of wealth is as equalized as anywhere in Asia. There are social classes, yet no hereditary aristocracy. Any person of ability can rise to the highest position in the nation.

The average Burman is a farmer or a fisherman. Only 15 per cent of the nation's population are urban, and but one third of Rangoon's citizens are Burmese. Rangoon, the one large city, has little connection with the culture and life of Burma, for the rural dweller is concerned with the metropolis only as a market for his goods and as a source of needed supplies.

BUDDHISM'S REVIVAL

Wartime conditions produced a revival of Buddhism, not as a world-denying but as a world-affirming gospel. The current revival comes out of the sufferings of the Burmese, traditionally Buddhists, who under the Japanese turned to the consolations of their religion. Unlike an earlier revival, the present resurgence of Buddhism is not anti-Christian. Rather, Prime Minister U Nu has urged Buddhists to become better Buddhists, Christians better Christians, and Muslims better Muslims.

Three sects of Buddhism claim 95 per cent of the people as adherents. They insist that since Christianity has brought on so many wars during the past nineteen centuries, Buddhism must now extend itself with its gospel of peace. The propaganda is government financed. The Peace Pagoda, for instance, is referred to as "Nu's Pagoda."

While the Buddhist revival is not anti-Christian in intent or propaganda, statistics may show a decline in the rate of Christian growth. The identification of Buddhism with Burman nationality complicates the life of a Christian nationalist. The constitution recognizes the special position of the Buddhist faith as the religion of the majority of the people of the country.

An assembly hall that can seat twenty thousand worshipers has been constructed atop a small hill on the outskirts of Rangoon. This assembly hall, which resembles a cave, was erected to house the Sixth World Buddhist Council, opened by the Prime Minister in May, 1954. The Council was to conclude in May, 1956, with a conference on the Buddhist faith. Sixty-five missionaries have been commissioned since 1946 by the Hill Tracts Buddhist Mission; Buddhist missionaries will hereafter take their gospel to the entire world.

A University of Buddhist Culture, with one of the world's best libraries, is being established. Funds have been contributed by the Ford Foundation. This university will share the hilltop with the Peace Pagoda and the auditorium. It will be a center for the world Buddhist movement.

THE CHURCH IN BURMA

The Second World War also precipitated a religious revival within Christianity. Christians, like Buddhists, have been stimulated by collective tragedy to a greater realization of the inherent values of their faith.

The Japanese occupation of Burma, which began shortly after the attack on Pearl Harbor, produced a crisis for the Christian churches. All foreign personnel had to flee. Foreign subsidy, which had gone almost exclusively to school support, opening new churches, and missionary salaries, was stopped. Burmese and other native Christian groups, under war's necessities, carried the economic load and accepted the responsibilities that the missionaries' withdrawal occasioned. Though survival through adversity rather than evangelistic gain characterized this dark period, the contemporary religious revival has developed as a result of the wartime experiences.

Christians confronted by the Japanese invaders united, if not organically, at least in spirit and fellowship. The Reverend G. P. Charles, general secretary of the Christian Council of Burma, cites the developments in the ancient capital, Pegu, as illustrative. The Baptist church building was bombed, and the Methodist church was despoiled by the invaders. The Methodist minister withdrew, and the Anglican priest was killed, leaving only the Baptist pastor and a Methodist woman evangelist to care for all the Protestants, using for worship the Anglican sanctuary, the only Protestant church building left standing.

THE CHRISTIAN CONSTITUENCY

Christians—including both Roman Catholics and Protestants—comprise approximately 2 per cent of the total population of 19 million. Roman Catholics number 131,000, and the Protestant Christian community is estimated to be 400,000. Baptists, whose churches are the outgrowth of work initiated by Adoniram Judson, are the largest Protestant group. Baptist congregations are made up predominantly of Karens. The Baptist foreign staff in 1954 was larger than that of all other Protestant bodies combined; the Baptist Burman staff was six times larger than the total of all other Protestant groups.

The Anglican communion, a constituent part of the Church of India, Pakistan, Burma, and Ceylon, is numerically second. The Methodists operate in the Buddhist areas, where progress is slow, and have a smaller membership. Two thirds of the Methodists are found in Upper Burma, where the British mission operates. The remaining one third in lower Burma form an Annual Conference, a unit of the Central Conference of Southeast Asia. The Assemblies of God, the Seventh-Day Adventists, and the Lakher Pioneer Mission (British) have communities of a few thousand each.

CIVIL WAR AND THE CHURCHES

When independence came in 1948, it brought in its wake war between the government and Communist bands and also between the government and the Karens. The Karens, dwellers in central and northern Burma, number only 15 per cent of the total population. For centuries, they had been at war periodically with the plains dwellers, fearing oppression by the Burmese, who comprise about 75 per cent of the population. The army established bases near Rangoon where Karens had settled; the latter had supplies of ammunition abandoned by retreating Japanese, and they had the best soldiers. In the earlier years, the British had created an army of Karens, Indians, and Kachins. Most of the officers were Karens. Today the Burman Army is 50 per cent Burmese, but the government had no indigenous army save a battalion of engineers with which to start.

The Burman Government agreed to the establishment of an autonomous Karen state within the Union of Burma, but the Karens are a people scattered over lower and central Burma. Only in the Salween Valley, in the small area around Papun, are they a majority. For many years a rift between Karens and Burmese had deepened; hence it was easy for Karen landowners in the rich Delta ricelands, who feared the government's socialist policies, to engineer a revolt. The Roman Catholics declared their allegiance to the government and urged Catholics to take no part in the insurrection.

Forty per cent of the Karens and most of their leaders are Protestants, a fact that brought suspicion upon all Protestants. Among the Burmese, only a fraction of one per cent are Protestants. The Protestants were thus alleged to be denationalized by their religion. Foreign missionaries, especially those from America, were accused of responsibility for this denationalization. Even the Anglican Bishops of Calcutta and Rangoon were detained in their places of residence on one occasion when scheduled to make an inspection tour, because a submarine had been reported offshore at the point they were to visit.

Prime Minister U Nu, at a party in Rangoon in 1954, expressed regret because of the misinformation that had implicated the Bishop of Rangoon and that for some time had alienated local feelings.

The size of the missionary staffs reflects the disadvantages inherited by the Americans as a consequence of the Karen rebellion. There are eighty-eight American Baptist, Methodist, and Salvation Army missionaries, and forty-one representing the Bible Churchmen's Missionary Society (Anglican). By contrast, there are 148 Roman Catholic priests, mostly European, more than all Protestant missionaries, with a community of but one third the size.

CHRISTIAN LEADERS OF BURMA

Here in Burma, as elsewhere, the most important fact in contemporary Christian history is not the church organization, not the church's institutions, not even the interdenominational work. The essential and unanswerable fact is the individual Christian. The Christian church in Burma is not numerically large, but it possesses influential and attractive personalities as members. Men and women from the Burma Christian community have visited far countries and have made their impression upon other racial groups overseas. This was particularly true in England, because of the earlier political tie. It also proved true during wartime when a Christian from Burma accompanied some missionaries and Chinese Christians up the dangerous Burma Road, entered the back door of China, and spent many weeks preaching and teaching in the areas of China not held by Japanese troops.

But let one of today's Christian leaders be introduced more personally and in greater detail. A friend's letter reads in part, "The wonderful twinkle in her eyes and her sense of humor that has helped carry her through the hardest times are part of her essential self. Her home is a very happy one and she is a delightful hostess. . . . Her sheer courage, when she volunteered to go out into the armed area and try to negotiate with the revolution's leaders, was outstanding. She told me that it had been a revelation of God's real presence with her that she had actually felt no fear."

Mrs. Ba Maung Chain is the one about whom this sketch is written. Daughter of the late Sir San Crombie Po, M.D., she is from wonderful stock. Her great-grandfather was one of the earliest converts, so she is a fourth-generation Christian. Her father was the first Karen to get his education in America by his own efforts. After some years as an American citizen, he returned to Burma and spent the rest of his life in service to his people. He was undisputed leader of the Karens during his lifetime and, among many honors, he was knighted by the King of England. Mrs. Ba Maung Chain's one sister became a nurse, working with her father. Her five brothers have been distinguished in law, journalism, the army, and medicine.

She married Saw Ba Maung Chain, also a Karen Christian, an official in the Public Works Department of the Government of Burma. Since her marriage, she has found time and energy, in addition to what was needed for her home and the children, to help in church activities, in social welfare work, and in politics.

She worked faithfully in her own congregation and soon was a member of various wider organizations such as the Burma Baptist Convention and the interdenominational

Christian Council of Burma. She was the first woman to be elected president of this Council. She poured her strength into the work of the Y.W.C.A., becoming president of the Burma Y and a vice-president of the international Y.W.C.A. Deeply patriotic, she busied herself in the affairs of the new nation. She was elected a member of Parliament and was shortly appointed Minister of Karen Affairs, the first woman to be in the cabinet of Burma. Later she resigned this post in order to be freer to serve her people and her church.

In this small but strategically placed land, and in the small but devoted Christian church of that land, she stands out not only as a leader but typical of what the religion of Jesus Christ can and does accomplish for womanhood.[1]

CHRISTIAN COOPERATION

The churches, the mission bodies, the Bible Society, Y.M.C.A., Y.W.C.A., Christian Literature Society, and the Student Christian Movement maintain nationwide cooperation through the Christian Council of Burma, which was founded thirty years ago. Christian youth is organized in two national bodies, each of which performs a distinctive service. The Burmese Christian Youth Council is a representative body composed of delegates from the several churches and Christian organizations; the Burma Christian Youth League is an interdenominational, interracial body composed of independent members. The Y.M.C.A. and Y.W.C.A. reach the non-Christian communities with educational and social programs.

[1] A full life story of Mrs. Ba Maung Chain is soon to be published, the work of the Rev. Erville E. Sowards, an American Baptist missionary in Burma.

Theological education is provided in twelve Bible schools and one seminary. The Baptists operate a divinity school at Insein, near Rangoon. Holy Cross Seminary at Rangoon is used as a hostel for university students. Four hundred seventy-eight ordained ministers and 1,158 unordained evangelists serve the 1,883 local congregations. More than 40,000 Sunday school pupils are organized in eight hundred Sunday schools.

One of the outstanding achievements of the church is in the field of publishing and distributing Christian books and pamphlets. The Literature Committee of the Christian Council of Burma published thirteen titles and reprinted seven others in 1953, in a total of five different languages. Twelve of the publications were in Burmese. Individual denominations also work in this field.

Missionary funds are used to undergird Christian medical work, literature production, the operation of mobile units, and extension. The expenses of local congregations are primarily the responsibility of Burman Christians.

In prewar Burma, Christian schools and hospitals were an important aspect of the Christian program. The missionaries felt obliged to provide instruction for the first converts. The Morton Lane-Judson School in Moulmein, dating back to 1834, Kemmendine in Rangoon, and Mandalay Girl's High and Normal Schools were Christian answers to the low value placed by Burmese Buddhism upon women. Rangoon College had been transformed by Elias William Kelly into Judson College. These institutions accepted state grants, following the logic that since the government had the responsibility to operate schools, cooperation in this obligation was one means of accomplishing the missionary purpose.

In the early thirties, governmental restrictions were placed upon religious instruction in those institutions.

Most of the schools under Christian auspices have been established among the Karens in villages wholly Christian, where the same men have provided leadership for the village schools and the village churches. There are 173 primary schools, 31 middle schools, and 28 high schools.

Randolph L. Howard prophesied accurately in 1931 that the rise of a nationalistic fervor, which stressed Burma for the Buddhists, would place the Christian schools at a disadvantage. The absorption of Judson College into the University of Rangoon terminated a historic institution. The government has not been willing to charter an intermediate college with which the Baptists hope to fill the educational gap.

The conversion of Burma into a welfare state, according to the program outlined at the Pyidawtha Conference in 1952, threatens to bring Christian educational institutions within the government welfare system. In 1953, there were more than six thousand state schools in operation, and the government was planning an additional thousand.

Nine Christian hospitals have survived under the new conditions. The Namkham Hospital made famous by Dr. Gordon Seagrave is now a private institution, though distinctly Christian in control and purpose. The Ellen Mitchell Memorial Hospital at Moulmein was opened by the Baptists in 1918. Nearby, a home for leprosy patients is operated in association with the World Mission to Lepers, with headquarters in London. A tuberculosis rest home is operating at Taunggyi. In general, the mission did not seek to compete with the government in areas where the latter adequately fulfilled its responsibility for medical care. Of the nine hospitals, four are operated by the Baptists, three by the Bible Churchmen's Missionary Society, and one each by the British Methodists and the Anglicans.

Burman Christians are accepting the revival of Buddhism as a stimulus to a more effective proclamation of the Christian gospel. In December, 1954, a month of nationwide evangelism was conducted, in which four hundred congregations participated. A call to the churches was distributed six months in advance. Two sets of correspondence courses in two different languages have been widely circulated. Non-Christians are purchasing four times the number of Bible portions they did in the prewar period. Local congregations have charge of their distribution. The Burman people, 50 to 60 per cent literate, are avid readers.

The Reverend A. J. Eastman, quoting the delegates to the 1953 Annual Meeting of the Christian Council of Burma, said:

The obstacles facing the church today are fast proving to be the source of her greatest opportunity. It was observed that both nationalism and the resurgence of Buddhism (which are too often made to be one and the same thing) have brought Christians to be recognized as fellow-citizens. The church has, furthermore, been awakened to self-examination and heart-searching. The task of training and using indigenous leadership has received priority, and the church is rapidly learning to depend much more upon its own resources than on those of the missions. As Christians find more and more ways of expressing their love for their country and their fellow men, the roots of the church are bound to sink deeper into the cultural soil of Burma. There may still be a long way to go, but the movement and the direction are certain.

CHAPTER 9

The Growing Fellowship

They may never have heard it, but a Filipino deacon or an Indonesian pastor would appreciate Benjamin Franklin's remark that the signers of the Declaration of Independence had better hang together, or they would hang separately. For if Christians in Southeast Asia are proud of their independence among the churches of the world, they are also aware of the interdependence of the churches in a world of conflicting forces.

Protestant churches in Asia are now a fact. They are self-governing, largely self-supporting, and they have the responsibility for extending the gospel. They may have received their independence before they were completely ready, but had they waited until they were completely ready before making the break with Western churches, the break might never have happened. We learn to be independent by being independent. After this lesson, though, comes another: there is no such thing as complete independence. The churches of Southeast Asia know that they are dependent on Christ, the Author of our faith and the Founder of the church. They also realize their dependency upon fellow Christians and sister churches in other lands, and the dependence of these men and churches on them.

Before World War II, the churches of Southeast Asia had few contacts with one another. Except at world conferences, where a few churchmen from the area met one another, there was little or no fellowship among their leaders. The lives of the churches had been closely linked with their parent bodies in the West. A Filipino Methodist was better acquainted with the work of the Methodists in distant America than he was with that in nearby Singapore. Educated Karens in Burma knew more about American Baptists than about the Chinese Baptist Church in Bangkok. This scarcity of information about one another existed despite the fact that the Southeast Asian churches faced many common problems.

POSTWAR CHANGES

The changes wrought since those prewar days are bringing a new kind of unity among Christian forces. The Bangkok Christian Conference of December, 1949, was arranged in no small measure by Asians and was led by them. The appointment of Asian secretaries by the World's Student Christian Federation, the World Alliance of the Y.M.C.A., and jointly by the International Missionary Council and the World Council of Churches has helped knit the Christian movements in this area.

Regional conferences were held at Manila in November, 1954, on home and family life; at Bangkok in March, 1955, on the use of audio-visual aids; at Bangkok in early 1956 on theological education. Gatherings such as these bring Christian workers together to share mutual experiences and problems. International work camps in Thailand and the Philippines, organized by the Youth Department of the World Council of Churches, gave the youth of Southeast Asia and adjacent Asian lands an opportunity to work and live together. The December, 1951, Conference of Christian Professors at Bandung, Java, sponsored by the World's Student Christian Federation, led the W.S.C.F. to encourage international exchange visits by Christian educators in Asia. Asian Christians are coming closer together today than ever before.

The experiences through which they are passing are roughly comparable to the Reformation period for European churches. Having freed themselves from foreign control (that of Rome), the Protestant churches then concentrated upon survival rather than upon missions. They consolidated and conserved their resources for 150 years before they felt sufficiently strong to reach beyond national borders. The churches of Asia, newly free from outside control, likewise will require a period of time for finding themselves. In Europe, the emphasis was upon national churches, as it is in Asia today. But in the case of the postwar churches of Asia, their national character is set in an ecumenical framework. This may prevent some of the Reformation excesses and also preclude an emphasis upon religious nationalism for its own sake.

THE PRESSING NEED FOR UNITY

The need for unity among the churches of Southeast Asia is particularly sharp because of problems of evangelism. Denominationalism promotes rugged individualism in religious belief and has added glow and warmth to religious life, but its divided witness confuses non-Christians. The tradition and heritage that justify each of the denominations in the lands of their birth are entirely lacking in Asia. Thus many of the separations are superficial. Generally, an Asian Christian is a Methodist or a Presbyterian or a Pentecostal according to the label of the missionary who converted him or his ancestors. Competition to make a Northern Thai into a Southern Baptist, or a Chinese of Malaya into an Anglican, must appear ludicrous to a Buddhist or a Muslim. The Japanese Christian, Toyohiko Kagawa, told a seminary audience in the United States, "When I was baptized, I thought I became a Christian; now that I am in America, I discover instead that I am a Presbyterian."

In recent years, numerous Christian sects, most of them small, have swarmed into every land of Asia. They observe no comity, nor do they cooperate with other Christians. These sects bring with them values of Christian faith and life that attract non-Christians. They have a passion for winning souls to Christ, but their divisive tactics tend to weaken the Christian witness and handicap the progress of Christianity. The church should unite rather than divide Christians in a part of the world that already has too many tendencies toward division. A highly-educated Indian ambassador has said that the "wide variety of Christian sects . . . each proclaiming the errors and superstitions of others, is a source of embarrassment to missionary work."

MOVEMENTS TOWARD UNITY

A measure of cooperation has been obtained in Thailand, Burma, and Malaya in National Christian Councils, in the Federation of Christian Churches in the Philippines, and in the Council of Churches in Indonesia. These bind together Christians of different church bodies, polities, and theologies in common projects of cooperation and witness. United churches have developed in several of these lands. The Church of Christ in Thailand embraces most of the Thai Protestants. The United Church of Christ in the Philippines includes all the major American bodies that operated among the Filipinos before the war, except the Methodists and Baptists. The Council of Churches in Indonesia has as its one stated aim the achievement of a united church of Christ, to be formed of the thirty member bodies. Christians in the West may regard church union as a luxury. In non-Christian Southeast Asia, it is a necessity.

For the average Asian Christian, the ecumenical movement, as exemplified by the World Council of Churches and the International Missionary Council, has a powerful attraction. He sees himself as a member of a world fellowship and no longer feels alone amid a multitude of non-Christian neighbors. He sees the churches coming together so that there may be a united witness to Christ. To choose between unity with all the Christians in his land, or with members of his confession, presents the average Christian with a difficult dilemma.

This yearning for fellowship among the Christians of Southeast Asia calls for understanding and encouragement from mission boards, churches, and individual Christians in the lands from which the gospel has been carried to Asia.

CHAPTER 10

The Church in the "Land of the Free"

Bangkok, Thailand, with temple domes of gilt and mosaic made from broken pottery, sluggish canals, well-fed people and wide-open opium dens, is probably the most exotic of all Asian capitals. A stable currency, internal peace, and a busy airport have made it the Geneva of the Far East. Most of the United Nations' organizations have located their Southeast Asian staffs in this city.

The export of a million tons of rice annually, American aid, Korean War prosperity, and the presence of many international officials, plus the coming of thousands of tourists whose pockets are lined with hard currency, have created a kind of prosperity in Thailand. This is limited, however, to the cities and to only part of the cities' populations.

The farmers till their fields. The canals rise and fall with the tides. For the masses, so largely rural, life is basically the same as it was under the ancient kings. As goes Southeast Asia, so goes Thailand, and no people are more likely to ride the waves than are the Thai. Free in name only, they go their ways unconcerned by political changes and coups, because they are well fed.

The land is kite shaped, the northern boundary partly parallel with Burma and the southern reaching almost to the Malayan seaport, Penang. The area, 200,000 square miles, is roughly equal to the combined size of New England, New York, New Jersey, Pennsylvania, and West Virginia. It supports a population of nineteen and a half million.

The religious climate in which the Christian churches must work is a strange mixture. On the whole it is ambiguous. The people around Bangkok are Buddhist. While the Constitution grants religious freedom, the king must be a Buddhist. In the peninsula, the Thai people shade off into Malays, who are Muslim in religion. Northward into the hills, the animist tribes still abound. The king's religious authority and his political authority alike are still somewhat nebulous.

Puang Pibul-Songgram, the premier, was a wartime ally of Japan. After a short time out of office, he returned to power, and today is politically on the side of the free world, as opposed to the attitude of the neutralists in neighboring countries. In a series of coups d'état he has strengthened his power at the expense of recent constitutional gains.

The ambiguous political and religious character of the nation is reflected in the people. They are charming, gracious, clean. Their continued existence is conditional upon the juxtaposition of forces over which they have little control. Few Thai are willing to discuss politics, internal or foreign. This appears to be an unconscious lack of interest, which undoubtedly reflects centuries of responding to the inevitables of existing situations.

In an area where other nations are experiencing the birth pangs of freedom and self rule, Thailand stands alone. It is the one country in which a foreign tourist or student can travel the length and breadth of the country without fear. Cobras and an occasional tiger may cause trouble; the enemies are not two-footed ones who carry Bren guns. The fact that its rice fields, rubber trees, teak forests, and tin mines were scarcely touched by the war has enabled this land to provide many of the resources needed for the rehabilitation of the rest of Asia.

Thailand resembles Switzerland not only in that it has remained an island of peace and prosperity during two wars that have devastated the neighboring countries, but also because it is today the headquarters of international organizations functioning for the United Nations. The United States also has extensive operations in Thailand, and it is accused in certain quarters of undergirding a weak regime that might otherwise fall. The facts are, however, that the United States' and United Nations' methods of operation require that they function through existing governments. The various aid schemes for Thailand are aimed at keeping the country on its economic feet, aiding in social development, and raising the Thai standard of living.

The Chinese community is one of Thailand's greatest internal problems. There are at least three million Chinese, approximately one sixth of the total population. One half of these retain Chinese citizenship. Even among government officials, Chinese blood is common. Many of the leaders in the Christian movement have Chinese names as well as Chinese blood.

In such a land and among such people, Christian churches have been planted and nourished by missionaries from the Western world.

EARLY EFFORTS OF MISSIONS

Protestant missionary work goes back as far as 1828. French Catholic missionaries first arrived in the tenth century. Christian progress among the Buddhists on the plains has been slow, and has been only slightly more encouraging among the hill tribes. The Roman Catholic Church numbers but 53,000, and the Protestant community approximates 30,000.

Six of the first Protestant agencies that worked in Thailand abandoned their efforts. The reasons were various. The six were: the Netherlands Missionary Society, the London Missionary Society, the American Board of Commissioners for Foreign Missions, the American Missionary Association, the American Baptist Foreign Missionary Society, which reopened work in 1952, and the Society for the Propagation of the Gospel.

The Church of Christ in Thailand is largely the outgrowth of the American Presbyterian work that began in Thailand in 1840, but includes churches that have grown out of the mission work of other denominational groups as well.

CHRISTIANITY IN WARTIME

When the Japanese subdued Thailand in 1941 and the Thai Government bowed to terms of the conquerors, the Thai church became a central fact in the lives of believers. The Japanese opposition to Christianity in Thailand forced the Thai to depend upon their own resources, spiritual and material. They survived, but not without scars. Whenever churches were occupied by troops, congregations worshiped in private homes. Christian schools continued to operate, though in only a single one were teachers permitted to offer Christian instruction.

The General Assembly of the Church of Christ in Thailand met every year during the occupation save in 1945, when bombings prevented. When Christian and Missionary Alliance missionaries were excluded, Thai ministers and workers of the Church of Christ helped keep the CMA congregations alive, including those inside territories of Indochina occupied by Thai troops. The church raised funds to aid Christian schools destroyed in the bombings and to purchase medicines for sick soldiers. Two booklets designed to undergird religion in the home were published by the church and distributed widely through the congregations. All of the seventy congregations were kept mutually in touch, by messages and by personal messengers. One single congregation, which had supported two evangelists before the Japanese occupation, supported eight during the years of crisis.

THE MANY MISSIONS OF THE CHURCH TODAY

Following the close of the war in the Pacific basin, missionary groups renewed their efforts in this land. It has been said that "next to Taiwan (Formosa), Thailand has become the open field for more mission groups than any other Asian country."

The British Churches of Christ Mission has recently been strengthened by the American Disciples of Christ. Two fraternal workers of the United Church of Christ in the Philippines, assigned to the Church of Christ in Thailand, are located in the station with the Disciples of Christ workers, where Thai, British, Filipino, and American missionaries work side by side.

The American Baptists re-entered Thailand in 1952 at the bidding of the Presbyterian Mission, U.S.A. They are working among the Swatow-speaking Chinese and the Karens on the Thai-Burma border.

The two-hundred-year-old Marburger Mission of Germany is working as an integral part of the Church of Christ in Thailand, with staff assigned to the church of Chiengrai.

Outside the Church of Christ in Thailand, but operating in comity, is the Christian and Missionary Alliance that entered via the French Indochina border, reaching out to the Lao tribes. The CMA carries responsibility in nineteen eastern provinces.

The World-Wide Evangelization Crusade has been pioneering since 1947 in an area released by the Presbyterian Mission.

The Overseas Missionary Fellowship (China Inland Mission) has a staff of sixty among Muslims in the southern peninsula, among the tribes in the North, in West-Central Thailand, and serving in several undermanned hospitals of the Church of Christ in Thailand. They plan in time to have a foreign staff of at least a hundred in Thailand. The New Tribes Mission is working west of Chiengrai, in the hills.

The Southern Baptists, when they entered in 1949, were welcomed by the Church of Christ but entered into no formal relationship with it. They have stations in Bangkok and in the ancient capital of Ayudhya.

Seventh-Day Adventists have operated a mission since 1918. Jehovah's Witnesses are both strong and aggressive.

EVIDENCES OF CHURCH STRENGTH

The Church of Christ in Thailand was formally organized in 1934. The government gradually has been giving it *de facto* recognition as an indigenous loyal body of Thai Christians. Responsibilities formerly carried by the mission are being borne by the church. The per capita subsidy that the Thai Government makes to Buddhists and Muslims is also made to Christians. In 1954, at the express wish of the government and with the approval of the Roman Catholics and the Seventh-Day Adventists, the Christian subsidy was transmitted through the Church of Christ in Thailand. The Foundation of the Church of Christ in Thailand is empowered under law to purchase, own, and sell property in the name of and for the entire church.

Viewed statistically, the Thai Christian community is weak, yet in no Asian land does Protestant Christianity have more prestige. The former king, Prajadhipok, loaned his private garden to the church for three days during the hundredth anniversary celebrations marking Protestant Christianity's beginnings in Thailand. The Regent, in the King's absence, personally opened the East Asia Conference of the International Missionary Council and World Council of Churches in December, 1949. Christian schools are patronized by government officials, and missionaries have served as tutors to future kings. High government officials are readily accessible to Protestant church leaders and Western missionaries, to a degree that is rare in other Southeast Asian lands.

The fact that only a relatively small percentage of Protestants have been won from among the Buddhist Thai may contribute to Protestantism's favorable position. The government realizes that the Christian church offers at present no real competition to official Buddhism. Christian schools and hospitals are assets to the nation, for which the only price is religious toleration.

Protestantism's status derives from the unique services rendered by the church and missions over the years. Missionaries introduced modern medicine, including inoculation against smallpox. Modern education and the printing press were brought in by Christian workers from the West. Although the government now operates schools, officials still enroll their own children in mission preparatory schools before sending them to a university.

Dr. Edward Charles Cort, who was from 1908 to 1949 associated with McCormick Hospital in Chiengmai, was decorated by the throne in recognition of his services. In 1940, the royal family established a ward in memory of H.R.H. Prince Mahidol of Songkhla. McKean Leprosy Colony, located nearby, is one of the finest medical projects in all Asia. It is supported jointly by the government and American Leprosy Missions, Inc.

Christianity has made an ethical and moral impact through sixteen schools and eight hospitals operated by the Church of Christ and its affiliated missions. One of the princesses said, "All that I am, I owe to my education at Wattana Wittaya" (a Presbyterian school for girls). But she remains an ardent Buddhist. Prominent Thai officials would defend the right of the church to operate its various institutions, but they and their children remain either practicing or nominal Buddhists.

Christianity's influence has been more by social permeation than by organic growth. There are few Christians in public positions, in government or on university staffs. There is no bloc of Protestants, as in the Philippines and Indonesia, who through their integrity and courage serve as the national conscience.

Postwar efforts on the part of the church and the Presbyterian Mission to establish a Christian university have been unavailing. (Bangkok College and Prince Royal's College are only preparatory schools.) The government has never permitted the establishment of a private university or granted a charter to a body with such a program.

The refusal of the government to charter such a university has led the church and mission jointly to establish a student center and hostel in Bangkok, which resembles church foundations located near state and private universities in the United States. The resident director and his wife operate a wide program of religious and social activities designed to attract and influence the Thai students enrolled in the several government universities.

The McGilvary Theological Seminary in Chiengmai, with three professors, graduated the first postwar class of five in 1952. Few students apply for matriculation. Out of thirty-five ordained ministers in the Church of Christ in Thailand, only eight are high school graduates. Most congregations appear satisfied with the services of an unordained preacher instead of an ordained minister to whom a salary must be paid. There is a Chinese language Bible school in Bangkok where Chinese women are trained.

The Church of Christ in Thailand and the Presbyterian Mission jointly have established a mechanized cooperative farm at Chiengrai in the North. The low density of population in this area permits homesteading of thirty acres per family. The Christians seek by the use of machinery to demonstrate that the agricultural yield per capita can be increased. Fifty families previously living as tenants were selected on the basis of their occupations. These included schoolteaching, carpentry, mechanical work, and so on, as well as farming.

Each family staked out the maximum area allowed. Temporary houses for men were later replaced by more substantial homes into which families were moved. A church and a school were built of bamboo and thatch, with dirt floors. At the end of three years, all who had spent the allotted time on the farm were given title, which they could sell, but only back to the cooperative.

The cooperative does not expect to recoup the investment in tractors and other modern agricultural equipment. The Christian community is seeking to speak through this experiment to the rural people, offering a working reality to meet the challenge of Communist promises.

A vigorous youth movement characterizes the postwar church in Thailand. Even before the missionaries returned in February, 1946, six students at Bangkok Christian College organized themselves into a Christian Endeavor, the program of which included street preaching by the students as well as worship services and Bible study in the college. This pattern of organization spread to other schools and churches, with the result that in most of the congregations and sixteen Christian schools a youth fellowship has been started, primarily student led, but with adult guidance.

A program of work camps enables the Thai youth, in the words of the Reverend Horace W. Ryburn, to "work together, play together, worship together, and share their longings with sympathetic and wise counselors." The first international camp was held in the summer of 1951 at the Chiengrai farm. It was attended by Japanese, Filipino, Malayan, Burman, and Thai youth. They laid the foundation of a storehouse and helped clear jungle land.

CHAPTER 11

The Churches in Indonesia

Without some knowledge of the historical and political setting in Indonesia, the reader can understand only sketchily the country's Christian movement. This is true of all Asian countries, but is particularly—almost tragically—true of the far-flung islands making up the Republic of Indonesia.

THE NETHERLANDS EAST INDIES (INDONESIA)

After the Dutch took over the area about 1600, the other nations in the West paid scant attention to this string of islands, save for the period about 1812, when Great Britain temporarily ruled them. For three and a half centuries, Holland governed these peoples, to the economic advantage of the Dutch merchants and of the Chinese who were introduced by the colonial government as middlemen.

The Dutch provided some education, roads, and transportation. They made no effort to change the cultural patterns of Indonesian life. But they made one basic mistake: they treated the Indonesians as children. The Dutch masters could not imagine that these diverse peoples, scattered over an area of land and water vaster than the United States, and speaking more than two hundred languages, would ever want to be free of Dutch rule. Only 6 per cent learned to read. Even minor government positions were filled by Dutch personnel, and Indonesians who manifested an interest in politics were imprisoned.

When the Japanese occupied the islands in February, 1942, some Indonesians were taken from concentration camps and for the first time in their lives were given government positions. They liked it so well that, when the Japanese surrendered in 1945, the Indonesians then governing insisted upon remaining in power.

A bloody war ensued between Dutch and Indonesians, which culminated in United Nations intervention. After a cease-fire was agreed upon, two military actions initiated by the Dutch forces forfeited most of the good will that their previous benevolent colonial rule had created. The animosity that the Indonesians have for their former masters is matched in Asia only by that of the Viet Minh against the French. The tensions between Dutch and Indonesians are a handicap to the development of this young republic of Asia.

To understand the influence of communism in Indonesia, we must feel the population pressure on Java, the low income, and the frustrations that have come with independence. The vacuum created by loss of hope, the foreign control of many of Indonesia's resources, the country's position as a pawn in power politics, the long suspicion toward the white man, and the lack of economic and political stability provide an opening for any ideology or economic system.

Communism is adjusting its promises and program to meet these real needs. The spearheads of communism are segments of the large Chinese population (totaling three million), labor organizations, and the continuing unrest following the revolt against the Dutch.

Such a situation is unfortunate for Indonesia and for the world. This young republic is important. With a population estimated at 78 million, it is sixth in size among the nations. Oil, tin, rubber, and copra, which the islands have in abundance, make them a prize to be courted or taken by force. The hundreds of islands, including Sumatra, Java, South Borneo, Celebes, the Moluccas, and the Lesser Sundas, reach from east to west for more than three thousand miles.

President Sukarno, still a young and vigorous man, said at one time that the Indonesian people will not go Communist if they remain contented.

"How can they be kept contented?" he was asked.

"By having what they need to eat and what they need to develop their country."

"How will you be able to satisfy these demands?"

His answer was the same one given by each of the younger nations: "We must industrialize, and to industrialize we must have outside assistance."

His logic is inescapable. Many of the 125 Americans working in the International Cooperation Administration Program are aiding in this industrialization process, though the former American Ambassador reportedly insisted that aid should be primarily for the improvement of agriculture —which also is needed, for Indonesia in 1951 had to import 600,000 tons of rice. The government expected to be self-sufficient in rice production by 1955. Under freedom, peasants who formerly ate potatoes and other rice substitutes insist upon eating rice, as do the members of the middle and upper classes.

More than one half of the Indonesian population lives on Java, which is but 11 per cent of the land area. Java is also the home of the revolution and today provides the nation with most of its political leaders. Tensions thus develop between Java and other parts of the country that threaten the very existence of the nation.

The three thousand islands are the home of more than two hundred linguistic groups, yet a variety of Malay is becoming the national language. Save on Bali, Islam is the prevailing religion, though it has been moderated by Javanese mysticism and Malay pragmatic good sense.

WHAT ABOUT THE CHURCHES?

The so-called "independent foreign policy" followed by government is the prism through which every event and idea is refracted and analyzed in Indonesia today. Directly and indirectly, the attitudes inherent in this policy function in the ecclesiastical world as well as in the political. Any gift from a foreign source is eyed with suspicion, lest there be strings attached. Neither church nor state wishes to be compromised by dependence upon non-Indonesian sources. Some churchmen feel it is better to accept gifts from a predominantly Muslim Indonesian Government than from Christian foreign sources.

The Indonesian Protestant community today numbers about five million. The largest body of ex-Muslim Christians (85,000) in the world is on Java. Prior to 1945, it was the one major mission field in Asia essentially unaffected by

American missionary enterprise. But American missionary societies are now working in Indonesia, both in cooperation with existing church bodies and outside them.

Thirty autonomous church bodies, numbering five thousand to 600,000 Christians each, constitute the National Council of Churches in Indonesia. These can be classified this way: (1) Indonesians; (2) Chinese; (3) Dutch; (4) mixed congregations of Indonesians, Europeans, Indo-Europeans, and Chinese. They also can be classified according to organizational origins: (1) the so-called Protestant Church of the Netherlands East Indies (Dutch), "established" until 1935 and having a state-paid ministry until 1950; (2) churches that developed from activities of voluntary mission societies, especially Dutch, German, Swiss, and American; (3) churches established through the missionary activities of Indonesian or Chinese-Indonesian churches. Most of them are church bodies holding the Reformed faith and theology.

Most of the larger church bodies in Indonesia have a mass movement history. Such movements took place primarily in animistic areas that were early reached by Christian missionaries and had not been touched by the earlier Islamic invasions. The Batak, Minahassa, and Timorese Churches are examples.

The movement of masses of animists into the Christian community continues. The major task of the churches in these areas is to Christianize the Christians, that is, through instruction, to nurture them into full church membership, and to hold Christian youth in the face of sectarianism and secular influences.

Other church bodies, particularly on Java, have been

created by converting Muslims, one by one, to Christianity. That method always has been slow. Today it is slower still, though Christian workers do report occasional requests from Muslims for instruction and even baptism.

Visitors with a background of Western denominationalism do not readily appreciate the racial, regional, linguistic, and cultural bases of the Indonesian church divisions. Save for the Gereformeerde (Free Secessionist) churches, differences of doctrine, orders, etc., are secondary. The divisions are derived from the comity that was enforced by the Netherlands East Indies Government, which allowed one missionary society to operate among the Indonesian population within a given geographical area. To be Christian is, to communicants in Indonesia, virtually synonymous with being a member of the particular church of one's own region or island.

GOVERNMENT AND THE CHURCH

The Protestant Church of the Netherlands East Indies was first established by the Dutch East Indies Company to minister to its Dutch officials and employees. Chaplains also extended their operations among the native peoples. When the company failed, responsibility for the church was assumed by the colonial government. Today four major church bodies representing different geographical areas are included within this church. These are the Christian Evangelical Church in Minahassa in Northeast Celebes, the Protestant Church of the Moluccas (sometimes called the Amboinese Church), the Christian Evangelical Church of Timor, and the Protestant Church in Western Indonesia. One third or more of the Protestants in Indonesia are embraced in these four large church bodies, the origins of which date back to 1607.

The colonial government formerly exercised supervision over all religious communities and groups. The civil officials determined which territories should have missionaries, the languages to be used in religious services, the schools to be opened, the salaries to be paid, and the personnel to be employed or assigned. From 1854, when all Protestant churches in the East Indies were merged by a royal decree, until 1927, any religious organization that did not work within the state-supported and established church or the Roman Catholic Church was treated merely as an ethical society. Voluntary missionary sending agencies that did not operate within the framework of the established church thus were forced to work without the protection of a legal position in the Indies until after 1927.

Roman Catholic priests were not segregated in their operation; that is, they worked without distinction among Europeans and Indonesians. Some ministers of the Protestant Church of the Netherlands East Indies ministered to Europeans and others to Asian Christians.

The church bodies with missionary origins date back to 1797 when the first voluntary society was organized in Holland to concentrate upon work among the people of Indonesia. Most of the ministers appointed to serve the Protestant Church and the early missionaries commissioned by the sending societies came from the Dutch Reformed Church.

But not all missionary effort has had its origin in Holland. The development of the Batak churches is the most important exception. Late one evening in the year 1832, two

Americans appeared at the outskirts of a village in Northwest Sumatra and announced that they had come to proclaim Christ. The villagers promptly seized them and put them to death.

When, several years later, German representatives of the Rhenish Missionary Society came for the same purpose, they were more fortunate. They remained alive to preach Christianity, and today more than 700,000 Bataks are members of several branches of the Christian church. Christianity has replaced the animism of times past as the cementing factor in community life. An annual day of repentance is observed for the brutal treatment of the first missionaries.

The H.K.B.P., as the major Batak church is popularly known, is the largest of the Indonesian regional church bodies. The mass movement of the Bataks into the church ranks with the growth of the Korean church and with the acceptance of the Christian faith by the Karens as one of the modern miracles of the gospel. The Batak church leaders have been given their education by the mission and the church.

Let us turn to another denomination. The Methodist Conference differs from most of the other autonomous church bodies in Indonesia, not so much with respect to theology and church order as in respect to (1) the position foreign missionaries have held in church organization and institutions, as district superintendents and principals of schools, (2) its organic relations with a church of another country (the United States), and (3) its biracial character, the membership being Chinese and Indonesian, as it is a merger of two racial conferences.

The churches in Indonesia have sent missionaries both

to unevangelized groups within their own areas of operation and to other unevangelized areas. The older and self-supporting congregations in the majority of the synods maintain preaching points where services are conducted by evangelists or visiting city ministers. The Protestant Church of the Moluccas has supported missionaries in Irian (West New Guinea), the Christian Evangelical Church in Minahassa in Luwuk, Banggai, and in Timor. The Chinese churches in Central Java were the outgrowth of missionary activity financed by the Dutch-language congregations of the Reformed churches in the area.

GOVERNMENT-SUPPORTED CHRISTIAN INSTITUTIONS

A government that could support an established church could easily justify subsidy for schools, hospitals, and social institutions established and administered under Christian auspices. More than 1,500 primary schools in Indonesia today are "Christian." That is, they were founded by the churches, though, with a few exceptions, most of the original cost was covered by the state. The teachers are Christian, or at least acceptable to the Christian administration, though their salaries are provided for in the school budgets and thus are covered by state subsidies and school fees.

Christian hospitals were established in the same manner, the government providing the bulk of construction funds and a liberal contribution toward budget. Foreign doctors and nurses for the staff were recruited in Europe by mission boards, but placed on the payroll of the hospital (as foreign teachers were provided for within the school budget).

MISSIONARIES FEW: CHRISTIAN
WORKERS MANY

In contrast with the many hundreds of foreign Christian workers in other Asian lands, the number of non-Asians appointed by sending societies as missionaries is relatively small. For example, today only six ordained missionaries are serving in the largest of the Batak churches, with more than 600,000 Christians, while in the 1920's there were forty. Similarly, Timor, with a Protestant community as large as that in Japan, has but three ordained missionaries working with the churches. A number of reasons explain the difference:

The strong Indonesian churches are the result of mass or village conversions. They never have had a staff sufficient to educate the converts to the meaning of Christian faith. In mass movement areas, baptism is easily obtained, but full church membership, with the right to partake of the Sacrament, is limited to those members who have undergone catechetical study and passed an examination. On Timor, such members number only approximately 8 per cent of the total membership. In many areas, the task of Christianizing the converts remains to be done.

Laymen have participated actively in the effort to convert the islanders. Government officials and businessmen from Holland in many instances were consecrated Evangelicals who gave generously of their time and energy to the work of the church. Notably the Neukirchen Mission that established itself in Central Java was initiated by plantation managers, ex-seamen, wives, and government officials, before an effort was made to recruit missionary assistance.

In the Chinese-speaking Chinese churches, the people still are dependent upon lay preaching and leadership.

Many of the foreign Christian workers engaged in distinctively Christian work were technically employed by hospitals, schools, and the government. Likewise the ministers of the state-supported Protestant Church of the Netherlands East Indies were technically employees of the state rather than of the mission boards in Holland.

NON-ASIAN INFLUENCE ON THE INDONESIAN CHURCH

The Protestantism that has taken root in Indonesia is primarily Dutch and secondarily German in origin. The four regional branches of the one-time established Protestant Church and eleven or more of the church bodies that have developed from missionary activities derive directly from the Nederlands Hervormde Kerk (Reformed Church of the Netherlands).

The second strongest influence in determining the character of Indonesian Protestantism is German. Workers of the Rhenish Missionary Society were instrumental in the conversion of the Bataks of West Sumatra and the nearby islanders of Nias. The World Lutheran Federation is now supplying the personnel and funds needed to maintain this large church.

Contrary to the situation in every other Asian land east of Afghanistan, the American influence in Indonesia is negligible. The Methodist Mission is the only world-wide agency that has been operating in Indonesia, specifically in Java and Sumatra. After 1928, by agreement with Dutch missions, operations were restricted to North and West Sumatra. The

American Protestant Episcopal Church worked among the Chinese in Djakarta (then Batavia) for a time.

A number of other agencies with staff recruited primarily from the United States are working in various parts of Indonesia. Largest of these is the Christian and Missionary Alliance, with more than fifty Western men and women on its staff, which is concentrating primarily upon the remote districts of Kalimantan (South Borneo). The Seventh-Day Adventists operate schools and hospitals on several of the islands, their largest work being among the already Christianized Menadonese in Northeast Celebes. A number of Pentecostal agencies operate city tabernacles and small meeting places. Many of their Western promoters are lay leaders who are in Indonesia as businessmen rather than registered as religious workers. Early in 1952, ex-China missionaries of the Southern Baptist Convention arrived on Java to work among the Chinese population. The Southeast Asia Committee of the Division of Foreign Missions of the National Council of the Churches of Christ in the United States of America has appointed a field administrator to serve in a liaison capacity between boards of missions in the United States and the National Council of Churches in Indonesia and its constituent bodies.

EFFORTS TOWARD UNITY

When these scattered islands achieved their political independence in 1945, Christians conceived the possibility of a parallel ecclesiastical development, that is, of establishing a united Protestant church of Indonesia. Following the work of a preparatory committee, delegates from twenty-eight autonomous church bodies met in Djakarta in May, 1950, and founded the National Council of Churches in Indonesia, the constitutional purpose of which is to achieve a single united Protestant church in Indonesia.

Among the many able Christian leaders are W. J. Rumambi and Simon Marantika. When the Japanese had ousted the Dutch from Indonesia, they asked the church to replace Western leaders who had been interned with some of its youngest men. Among the recent graduates of the Djakarta Theological College was the Reverend W. J. Rumambi of Minahassa. He was given a post of leadership and during the war years demonstrated his abilities. Mr. Rumambi, inspired by the Reverend A. Z. Wenas, a spiritual father of the church, set up the ideal of an ecumenical organization that would embrace the entire Christian community of Indonesia. One of the strongest regional councils today embraces the churches adjacent to Minahassa, where these men had lived.

At the close of the war, Rumambi located in Makassar, which became the capital of the State of Eastern Indonesia, and with this as a center, he organized the Council of Churches of Eastern Indonesia. When he removed to Djakarta, plans were begun to create the National Council of Churches in Indonesia. In May, 1950, came the formal organization, when Mr. Rumambi was named general secretary of the body.

In 1952, he attended the Willingen Conference of the International Missionary Council, together with the chairman of the National Council, Dr. S. G. T. Moelia. In 1954, he was called back to Minahassa to supervise the vast educational activities of the synod.

His successor, the Reverend Simon Marantika, is one of

the younger men to whom leadership was given after the collapse of the Dutch. Recently graduated from the Djakarta Theological College, he became head of the Protestant Church of the Moluccas, oldest of the Protestant church bodies in Indonesia. The congregations of this group are dispersed over a land and water area as large as the Philippine Islands. Early in 1950, he visited these isolated congregations. After his return from this trip, he was called upon to head the theological school of the church, in which more than fifty students were preparing for the ministry. With four other professors, he carried the four-year course and at the same time supplied leadership to the congregations and the church headquarters.

In the autumn of 1954, he was invited to become general secretary of the National Council of Churches in Indonesia. In this position, he is also chairman of the Ecumenical Youth Movement, Chairman of the National Missionary Commission (which in organization and function resembles the National Christian Councils of other Asian lands), and is the chief administrative officer of the Djakarta Theological College. He attended the Inter-Church Aid meetings of the World Council of Churches in Switzerland and in the United States.

As general secretary of the major ecumenical body in Indonesia, he travels widely among the constituent churches, seeking to create a mutual awareness of the widely dispersed Christian communities and to gain support for the ecumenical enterprises within the republic.

These men and their colleagues encountered numerous obstacles to church union. Fundamentally, the difficulty is geographical and ethnological. The islands are so many and so widely scattered, and the races and tribes with different languages and cultures so numerous that unification is all but hopelessly handicapped.

Too, there is a nationwide reaction against centralization. In essence, it is directed against the national government, but naturally the same spirit militates against church centralization.

The primacy of organizational survival is another obstacle. The several autonomous churches are forced to give major attention to self-support, the training of leadership, and the strengthening of their Christian witness in a predominantly Muslim, or Buddhist-Hindu, environment. Such herculean efforts have left little energy for ecumenical operations.

It is probably true that the slowness of devolution (the transfer of responsibility from the mission to the churches) contributes to the tardiness of the Indonesian churches in embracing ecumenicity. They had so little responsibility in the prewar period that their leaders are unprepared for visions of unity, either within Indonesia or in the world-wide Christian fellowship.

And yet—in spite of the handicaps to unity, in spite of considerable opposition to it, the unprejudiced observer recognizes with heartfelt praise the degree of progress made in the National Council of Churches in Indonesia and in the many examples of united Christian work. In a republic moving toward unity in the midst of political chaos and economic difficulties, in an atmosphere strongly Islamic or Buddhist-Hindu, and against the constant pressures of communism in both the Indonesian and Chinese populations, the Christians of Indonesia are making progress as churches and are moving toward unity.

CHAPTER 12

The Church in Indochina

Indochina stands second in population among the lands in Southeast Asia that we are discussing. Yet it is last in terms of Protestant missionary effort. Of the 27 million people, nearly 1,600,000 are Christians, the greater number Roman Catholics.

Indochina spotlights Protestantism's lack of an ordered or organized world strategy. Possibly intimidated by French colonial policy, the Reformed Church of France, operating in sixteen mission fields, made little effort to evangelize the peoples in this vast empire. It was also overlooked by the major European and American sending societies.

French rule extends back only about a century. This area has been the most profitable of all French colonies, which explains the reluctance of France to give the people their freedom or even to admit the end of colonialism in Asia.

The entire area known as Indochina is now divided into three associated states of the French Union—the National State of Viet Nam, Cambodia, and Laos—and the Democratic Republic of Viet Nam. The National State is usually referred to as South Viet Nam, and the Democratic Republic, which is, in fact, not democratic but communistic, is called North Viet Nam.

Like its neighbors, Indochina is primarily rural, 90 per cent of the people earning their living from the soil. In the delta near Saigon, up to six thousand rural people are living in each square mile (metropolitan Los Angeles averages but four thousand), though the average density of population in Indochina is much lower. The vast majority of the people are concentrated in about 50,000 square miles of rice-growing land. The largely mountainous nature of the land helps explain the ability of guerrilla bands to escape mopping-up operations of armies and police.

THREE FOREIGN INFLUENCES

French Influence. Such unity as is found in Indochina is not geographical, ethnic, nor linguistic, but political. Divided by climate, mountains, cultures, and origins, the people of this "Separated Big Toe," as the area was early named in Chinese records, were forced together by France.

Although French rule began at a comparatively recent date, France gained her initial foothold in Indochina in the late eighteenth century. The ruler of Cochin China, Nguyen phua Anh, a member of the powerful Nguyen family that had long been supreme in southern Annam, had been driven into exile in Siam (now Thailand) after a great rebellion. Through the Vicar Apostolic, Pigneau de Behaine, he appealed to the French for aid. In return for their military support and Nguyen phua Anh's restoration to his throne, the French asked for and received by treaty the port of Tourane on the Annam coast and the island of Poulo Condore in the Mekong Delta.

The French Revolution prevented the exploitation of these concessions until the British began to seek entrance into China. Then, in a series of actions similar to those executed by other imperialistic nations, France gained political control of the entire area.

Indian Influence. Cambodia evidences the remains of the Khmer Kingdom, once a major civilization that centered around the great lake of Tonle Sap. This area provided an overland route between the East and the West. It was here that Indian influence reached its zenith about the year 1000. The Khmer people, migrating from India, subdued large areas of Indonesia as well as Indochina, bringing Buddhism with them. Angkor was the center of their operations on the mainland, where they erected the great temple of Angkor Vat and other lasting monuments.

After reaching the prime of its cultural attainments, the Kingdom was assailed from two directions, in both cases by peoples who in turn were being driven south by the military movements of Kublai Khan around 1250. The Thai, who were pushed out of Southwest China, and the Annamese, who moved from the other side, squeezed Cambodia between pincers and gradually reduced the Kingdom in size and influence. It was the timely arrival of the French that prevented the complete annihilation of Cambodian life and art. Although most of the skill and initiative demonstrated in Angkor Vat has since disappeared, the people's attachment to Buddhism has remained.

Chinese Influence. Strong Chinese influences are to be found in Vietnam, and the blood of immigrants and Annamese has been mixed for two thousand years. Ancestor worship, which was introduced by Confucianism, is the dominant religion of the land. Writing was formerly in Chinese script.

Chinese soldiers were stationed in Tonkin and Annam as early as the third century B.C. In the eighteenth century, upper class refugees in political disfavor in China settled in Cochin China. Thus, it was that there came to the region men of education, learning, and competence, many of them having been officials of the Chinese court. As they were usually not accompanied by their families, they intermarried with the natives of the land. Offspring were originally treated as Chinese, but after 1829 they were classed as Annamese and permitted to have full civil rights, even being allowed to hold office.

Chinese influence has continued to be felt within recent years as, under French protection, Chinese have found it profitable to migrate as businessmen and as laborers on plantations and in mines.

INDOCHINA TODAY

Indochina cannot be considered one country today. Look at any recent map of Southeast Asia and you will see the complex divisions of the area. Tonkin is the region just south of China, narrowing as it extends south along the sea to the boundary of Annam, which is a strip hemmed in between a high mountain range and the South China Sea. Below Annam and forming the very tip of the peninsula is Cochin China. Now turn your attention to the far North. Back of the mountains, touching China and Burma on the northwest and bounded by the eastern line of Thailand, lies Laos. The other division of Indochina is Cambodia, a large and beautiful area, lying on both sides of the Mekong River and further enriched by a large lake surrounded by mountains.

The artificial line that divides Viet Nam into North and South places Tonkin and part of Annam in North Viet Nam; the remainder of Annam and all of Cochin China are in South Viet Nam. Cambodia and Laos are separate states.

South Viet Nam in October, 1955, concluded a plebiscite that repudiated the absentee king, Bao Dai, and elected as head of government the former premier, Ngo Dinh Diem. There are evidences of infiltration of the Viet Minh (Communists from the North), and there are other forces of nationalism and revolution that lead to sporadic eruptions of violence.

A reference to Chapter 5 will add details of the struggle between Communists and non-Communists in this war-harried land.

BUT WHAT OF THE CHURCH?

Inasmuch as Protestant missions were born in this immediate area, their late arrival in Indochina is not easily explained, even though it is true that the French authorities discouraged the entry of Protestant missionaries. Dutch Protestants were preaching to the Spice Islanders in the seventeenth century. William Carey landed in 1793 at Calcutta, just a thousand miles from Hanoi. In 1813, Adoniram Judson moved to Rangoon, 750 miles west of Hanoi. Malacca, 650 miles from Saigon, was occupied by Protestant missionaries the following year. Dutch and British missionaries were en route to the Philippines soon after the smoke of Admiral Dewey's guns had blown clear of Manila Bay.

Late and limited mission enterprise in Indochina resulted in a Christian community entirely inadequate to provide the Christian witness and ministry demanded by the chaos following the Japanese surrender. A hasty survey reveals that Swiss missionaries work in Buddhist territory, although progress has been slow. They report 452 persons baptized during a half century of work. The Reformed Church of France has a membership of about 10,000 among French officials and army personnel. Seventh-Day Adventists and Jehovah's Witnesses are other missionary agencies at work.

Apart from these scattered efforts, the Christian and Missionary Alliance alone is carrying the responsibility for the evangelization of this land. Even before 1900, leaders of this society considered entering Indochina, but not until 1911, when missionaries were sent from South China, was this plan consummated. Their work was interrupted by the outbreak of World War I. Most of the growth has been since 1918.

The French Colonial Government limited the Christian and Missionary Alliance activities to the cities of North and Central Annam. Only after a long period of proving themselves were the workers able to expand their operations to other parts of the colony. Cambodia was opened in 1922, Laos in 1929, and work among the Vietnamese tribes was begun in 1929.

In 1927, a national church of Viet Nam, the Eglise Evangélique (associated with the Christian and Missionary Alliance), was organized with its own administration. On January 1, 1953, this body listed 115 congregations with 68 ordained ministers and a baptized adult membership of 12,435, or a Christian community of about 30,000. Subsequently, separate administrations have been set up also for Cambodia, Laos, and the tribes of Viet Nam. On January 1, 1953, there were 116 Christian and Missionary Alliance missionaries in Indochina. There were also 265 nationals ministering to 342 congregations.

The church and mission operate six Bible schools where the native workers are trained. The non-institutional policy of the Christian and Missionary Alliance has limited the contacts of the Eglise Evangélique to those inhabitants of Indochina who attend church services and read Christian literature. There are no Christian hospitals or schools to attract non-believers.

Self-support among the Indochinese congregations has been expedited by the "ladder method" of Dr. R. A. Jaffray. Ten contributors are asked to provide one tenth of the minister's support. Each unit of ten members adds another ten until the entire amount is guaranteed. Some congregations with fewer than a hundred members have become self-supporting.

We turn from Indochina with an unanswered, perhaps unanswerable, question echoing in our minds. If Protestant missions had earlier and more adequately sought to enter this land and if government had permitted their entry, would the present condition be better? Certainly we of the West cannot point with pride to the record, save as regards the devotion and heroism of Christian individuals and groups. With this question haunting our consciences, our survey moves to an area where the picture is almost totally different from that in Indochina.

CHAPTER 13

Paradise Regained

The South Pacific of Robert Louis Stevenson, Somerset Maugham, and James A. Michener is an immense area that is roughly 95 per cent water and 5 per cent solid ground. The land, green and tropical, is in the form of ten thousand islands. From New Guinea, by far the largest island, north and east to Hawaii, the distance is about four thousand miles. In the minds of most Americans, it is the area of the swaying palms, beachcombing, and World War II battles.

The story of missionary work in the area is not as spectacular as other accounts of activities might be, yet it is a brave story and an honorable one. More than any other Westerner, the missionary has preserved the Pacific islands for the people who live on them. He has sought to keep the islands free of disease and their inhabitants free of slavery. He has fought the debauchery that, with disease and slavery, was brought by outsiders to decimate and sometimes ruin the islands.

Paul Hasluck, Australian minister for territories, was glad to link missionary with territorial policy in 1953: "The faith that impels the missionary and the cause which he serves are above the sphere of temporal government, but . . . in improving the health of the people, in raising their standard of living, adding to their skills, opening their minds, and raising the level of their vision, the mission and the government have common tasks. . . ."

South Sea romantics have so frequently pictured the missionary as a rather comical bigot that few onlookers have noted that there is a Christian South Pacific. One million of the four million islanders are adherents of some church community, with Protestants outnumbering Roman Catholics three to one.

The success of missionary work can be seen in another aspect, the extent to which the churches have become self-governing, self-supporting, and self-propagating. Christian islanders have, from the beginning, served as missionaries (many of them martyrs) to other island groups. They achieved a high degree of self-support even before World War II, when they were required to assume the responsibilities of governing their own churches.

For all their being in an area favored by mission boards—and thus heavily supplied with missionaries—the islands pose some peculiar problems. For example, the ten thousand islands are small and are limited in their ability to communicate with one another and with the outside world. As a result, missionaries gradually built up what amounts to a Christian navy. Some of the foremost missionary activity has been based on ships operated by the London Missionary Society and the American Board of Commissioners for Foreign Missions. Another difficulty also involves communications. The many languages that are spoken limit workers to a few villages or tribes. The Bible is available in part or in its entirety in 150 South Pacific languages; another fifty translations are in progress. At least three hundred more dialects must be reduced to writing if the people who know only these tongues are to be reached for Christ.

POSTWAR PROBLEMS

As in other areas, World War II was a time of testing for the Christian islanders. The Japanese occupation stimulated nationalistic feelings, enabled the Christians to demonstrate leadership capacities, and generally accelerated the movement toward autonomy.

The churches lost much property and many members and pastors. On islands held by the Japanese, thousands of men, women, and children were killed by bombings, Japanese and Allied. Thousands more died of hunger and malnutrition because the Japanese commandeered existing food supplies and drove the people into the bush. In some of the islands off New Guinea, at least one quarter of the total population perished.

The people were shaken in other ways. Village life in accord with primitive customs became humdrum after the excitement and independence of working on airstrips and serving as military supply carriers. Dreams of a coming messiah, common among primitive peoples who encounter sophisticated, technological civilizations, resulted in the growth of strange cults. Some of the people lived in expectation of shipments of goods and machinery that would ease their lives. Village life was reorganized here and there according to the army pattern. Immoral practices of the foreign visitors tended to undermine island custom and law and the Christian standards that many of the communities had accepted. The new riches, created by the wartime influx of money, goods, and employment, the inducements to leave one's village, the availability of alcohol and gambling—all have left their imprint upon the character and life of the people of the islands.

Some Christians lost their faith as a consequence, but on the whole, church people demonstrated a rare loyalty and faithfulness. The incident recorded in Henry P. Van Dusen's *They Found the Church There* was not isolated but typical. An American flyer said, "Because of missions, I was feasted and not feasted upon when I fell from the sky."

The alterations in village life and island economy have produced comparable changes in the life and organization of the churches. The people demanded and are demanding fuller participation in the Christian enterprise. The same thing is true in regard to relations between the people and the governments that rule their islands. Nationalism in the islands does not have as clamorous a voice as it does elsewhere in Southeast Asia, but it does have a voice.

SAMOA

Samoans, as far back as the 1920's, were calling on New Zealand for greater participation in governing themselves. After the Japanese surrender, Samoa brought her case for self-government before the United Nations, and in 1947, a UN mission recommended more control over local affairs. Eight years later, Samoan representatives were in Wellington, New Zealand, consulting with sixteen European representatives about further steps toward autonomy. A New Zealander's warning that "self-government must be reached by dignified, orderly, and careful steps," and not "in one wild leap," is far removed from the government's execution of Chief Tamasese in the 1920's for his participation in the revolt against New Zealand control.

Tonga, which is south of Samoa, is the only independent kingdom in all the South Pacific. Although under British protection, it has been free since 1845 and is the envy of other island peoples. The Tongan situation has been held up by the Samoans as an example of what they would like.

The natives of the Cook Islands, east of Tonga, have demanded more political rights and larger participation in local industry. Tahitians have organized into syndicates, and on one occasion sought to prevent French officials from disembarking at Papeete on the grounds that it was unnecessary to send out French civil servants to jobs that could be done by the natives.

In the field of Christianity, the postwar period has brought a change in the missionary's position as evangelist and the assumption of this responsibility by the church bodies. The churches of the South Pacific are not as strong as some other Christian bodies in Southeast Asia, but many of them have demonstrated that they can stand alone.

A wide difference exists between these churches in the extent to which authority has changed hands. In Samoa, where nationalism has produced a high sense of independence, there is a church capable of handling its own affairs. At the opposite end of the spectrum are New Guinea tribes, with Stone Age cultures, who must yet be reached physically as well as confronted with the gospel.

The Samoan Church (established by British Congregationalists) has been independent for more than a quarter century. The 63,000 members of this family are organized into more than three hundred congregations, with not enough ordained ministers to go round. The church operates five schools, including Malus Theological College. Every Samoan village has presiding over its church and school a graduate of this college. The church is governed by an assembly of 120 members. Discipline and church life are controlled by forty elders, with whom seven missionaries work. Since 1920, these missionaries have been supported by the local congregations. The church controls its own finances, and local pastors are entirely supported by the local congregations. Missionaries have been sent to Papua and to the Gilbert and Ellice Islands.

The Methodist Church of Samoa, founded by Methodist missionaries from England, has more than 13,000 persons in its community. It has full autonomy as an independent district in the New South Wales Conference, pays all its own workers, and builds and maintains all its own churches. The Mission Board of the Methodist Church in Australia acts as an advisory committee at the request of the Samoan Methodist Church.

In winning Samoa, Christianity has come to terms with pre-Christian practices. Sabbath observance is common, but old beliefs and ideas appear unaffected. Mission teachers replaced the village priests, and the *matais* (the families' intercessors with supernatural forces) became village church deacons. Distinctively Samoan native church organizations have resulted. The islanders support their churches devotedly and generously, but some observers feel they have only a weak grasp of spiritual affairs.

One Westerner wrote: "There is little virility of Christian character, or reality of Christian experience, nor is there the sense of the spiritual that is to be found in some less favored communities. There has been no indication of any impulse to produce a literature; no Samoan has yet written a book."

THE COOK ISLANDS

On the Cook Islands, the London Missionary Society Church has been self-governing and self-supporting since 1945. Village life is centered about the churches, which are controlled by the chiefs and the elders. Ministers are rotated every five years. Eleven thousand of the 16,000 inhabitants of the islands are inside the Protestant community. The New Testament was translated in 1836, and the Old Testament in 1851.

In the early days of missions, strict blue laws were enforced, and there was an eight o'clock curfew. The picture of life under missionary control in James Michener's *Return to Paradise* was a fair representation of the theocratic control imposed on these islands a century ago. Today, with that control gone, the church is having the same trouble with its youth that Michener's fictional Mr. Morgan had with his own daughter. It is experiencing difficulties in holding the young people who travel or have extensive contacts with the Western communities.

THE FIJI ISLANDS

The Methodist Church in Fiji has 123,411 adherents of whom about a fourth are adult members. Here's a chunk of statistics: There are 620 congregations under the care of 138 ordained Fijian ministers, 518 catechists, and 5,432 local volunteer preachers. Seven thousand and seventy-five women class leaders conduct religious education groups. Twenty-three thousand, nine hundred and forty-seven pupils study in 508 Sunday schools, using materials prepared by a Board of Christian Education. Interestingly enough, the 10,000 Christian youth are organized into groups after the pattern of the American Methodist Youth Fellowships. The reason is that Setareki Tuilivoni, the only American-trained pastor, is giving full time to developing a youth fellowship patterned on the groups he observed in the American churches.

The churches operate a theological school, and ministerial students are required to take courses at an agricultural school that is also church run. The Central Medical College at Suva includes among its students many who are Christians from other islands.

On a map, the Fijis lie close to the International Date Line. Tahitians brought the gospel there in 1850, and British missionaries and Tongan Christians arrived five years later. Christianity was adopted by some Fijian leaders who extended its influence by force of arms.

The Fijians are fervent and devout in their religion. Gradually all authority in the churches is being turned over to Fijians, though the district superintendents are Australian missionaries. In many cases, the pastor of a church is also the local chief. More than three hundred Fijian missionaries have been sent out to the aborigines of North Australia, New Guinea, and the Solomons. Despite this impressive work, many of the Fijians are in need of a revitalized faith. Their church leaders are aware of this and are seeking to achieve it.

THE TONGA ISLANDS

The Protestant community on the Tonga Islands takes in most of the 49,000 inhabitants. Nearly half are in the Free Wesleyan Church; the remainder belong to the Church of Tonga and the Free Church of Tonga. These latter two churches resulted from splits in the parent body, which were caused not by theological differences, but by struggles for power.

To restrict the entrance of new sectarians who would take advantage of the religious liberty provisions of the constitution, foreign missionaries are limited to one per two thousand adherents. The churches have become self-governing, self-supporting, and self-propagating, but they still look to Western missionaries for leadership and advice. The church has the Bible and a large hymnal in the Tongan language.

TAHITI

Tahiti, which is far to the east of Tonga, attracted the concern of Christians by a strange twist of history. The famous mutiny on H.M.S. *Bounty* in 1788 focused so much public attention on the area that the London Missionary Society was formed to begin operations there. Later, the society's work in French Oceania was turned over to the Paris Evangelical Missionary Society. When France annexed the islands, almost one half of the inhabitants were Protestants. Today they are cared for by their own pastors and teachers. The Tahitian Bible, which was published in 1838, was the first Bible to be printed in any of the South Sea languages.

THE GILBERT ISLANDS, NEW CALEDONIA, AND NEW HEBRIDES

The London Missionary Society Church of the Gilbert Islands takes in more than one half of the 30,000 inhabitants of those islands. They, too, provide their own leadership.

In New Caledonia and its dependencies, which are relatively close to Australia, half the people are members of churches established by the London Missionary Society and shepherded by the Paris Society since 1869. The churches have their own ministers and teachers. Twenty or more languages are spoken; the Scriptures have been translated into only two of them. The churches still depend on missionary direction. The dollar prosperity of the war created social unrest and agitation for more self-government.

To the east and north are the New Hebrides, where responsibility is carried by the Presbyterian Church of Australia and the J. G. Paton Mission. There also is an autonomous Presbyterian Church. Protestants constitute about one third the population of about 50,000.

It was on one of the islands of this chain that the Jon Frum Movement developed. This nationalistic, anti-mission, and often anti-Christian activity set back the development of the church. It was provoked by administrative injustice and unscrupulous commercial dealings; nowhere else was slave-kidnapping worse than in the New Hebrides.

THE SOLOMON ISLANDS

Guadalcanal and the names of other Solomon Islands were imprinted on American minds because of the bloody battles fought there during World War II. The Anglican

Church, which has taken the lead in working among the Solomon Islanders, claims the loyalty of more than 30,000, which is about a third of the population. Other Christians are connected with the South Seas Evangelical Mission and the Methodists. The Anglican program has developed a brotherhood of chastity, poverty, and obedience, founded in 1925 by Ini Kopuria, to evangelize the jungle areas. A group called Friends of the Brothers supply food and beds for these pioneering expeditions. While not yet self-supporting or self-governing, the Solomons church is developing native leadership. Seventy-two languages are spoken in the islands, but in only nineteen have portions of the Bible been translated. There is a complete Bible in only one of the languages.

NEW GUINEA

On New Guinea, the second largest island in the world, are found extremes of heat and cold, ranging from malaria-infested swamps to snow-capped mountains. Men live today in the interior as did their ancestors in the Stone Age. The island reaches from east to west 1,500 miles, and is four hundred miles north to south. Part of it is governed by Australia; the western half, known as Irian, is claimed both by Holland and Indonesia.

In Northeast New Guinea, Lutherans have established what is the largest church body in the South Pacific, a community of more than 200,000 members. The work was begun in 1886 at Simbang near Finschhafen and grew rapidly. Christian colonists, often new converts, would settle in a pagan area and give a living demonstration of the Christian faith. Then an approach was made to the pagan community as a whole in an effort to obtain a favorable attitude toward Christianity.

Every effort was made to convert the individual to a dynamic faith in Christ under the operation of the Holy Spirit. The emphasis upon the responsibility of converts to share their newly found faith led many of them to become missionaries to neighboring tribes. Church structures were and are built by the people with whatever materials the members can supply; they are not erected by the mission.

The war interrupted missionary activities, but today there are twenty major mission stations and an equal number of schools. Three seminaries, staffed by European teachers, are attended by about two hundred students. Nineteen volunteer workers sent out by the Luther League, American Lutheran Youth Organization, helped repair the ravages of war.

In the Bismarck Archipelago, which is a part of the Mandated Territory, the Methodist Missionary Society of Australia has about 100,000 members gathered into nearly six hundred churches. Eleven thousand members lost their lives from starvation during the war. At Rabaul, the capital until earthquakes made it unsafe, a Chinese Methodist minister established a church community that is one of the few places in the entire South Seas where the Chinese have been brought effectively into the Christian program.

Approximately 40 per cent of the population of Papua, southeastern New Guinea, is Christian. There are more than 100,000 Protestants and 20,000 Roman Catholics. The London Missionary Society and the Methodist missionaries operate colleges that have turned out hundreds of ordained pastors, teachers, and lay workers.

Irian, the Indonesian name for that part of New Guinea west of the 141st meridian, is undeveloped compared with the remainder of the island. Though the Dutch have claimed the 150,000 square miles since 1823, they have established but six public schools and built but fifty miles of roads. Mission work among the one million inhabitants has been difficult; at one time it was said that there were more graves of missionaries than converts.

In the twentieth century, progress has been more rapid. The Netherlands Reformed Church claims a community of 87,500. The Church of the South Moluccas claims that 100,-000 of its members are in Irian, located primarily in the West and along the southern coast. Hundreds of Amboinese teachers are instructors in the mission schools. The Christian and Missionary Alliance has recently stationed missionaries in the interior, making use of a mountain lake as a landing place for planes. Several pilots have lost their lives in missionary service, providing communications between the bases and stations in New Guinea.

THE VOICE OF THE PEOPLE

One of the charges made against South Sea missions is that they have competed unfairly with private enterprise. R. W. Robson, editor of the *Pacific Islands Yearbook,* has answered that, while missions build, plant, and trade, they do so not for profit but to make the Christian operations self-supporting and self-contained. The wartime survival of much Christian work in the South Pacific was due to the sound economic base of the missions. The Roman Catholics and the Kwato mission conduct big trading operations. The Methodists operate small plantations and run specialized missions to teach the people agricultural production. The Kwato mission builds boats. The danger of such activities is that earning an income may take precedence over the religious attitudes that the Christian enterprise is supposed to engender. Native cooperatives have developed extensively since the war, especially in New Guinea and Papua.

The Reverend A. R. Tippett, historian of the Fijian Church, has written words that can be used to summarize the state of Christianity in the entire South Pacific. He says that from 1848, when the first Pacific Islander was admitted to the missionary circle, the people have had a say in the affairs of the church. One Western missionary was killed and eaten—but thousands of Fijians were killed for their faith. If the Westerner translated the Gospels, the islanders themselves circulated the books. If the missionary planned an organization, it was the island teacher who established it. If the Fijian church raises its voice, it is not the Western missionary's voice. Rather it is the debated opinion of the most representative body in the islands, a body composed of Fijian Christians with but a handful of whites.

The paradise of the Pacific is indeed being regained for Christ and his church.

CHAPTER 14

Ten Million Outsiders

Walking the streets and fields of Southeast Asia are more than 10 million people from India and China. These Indians and Chinese are problems to themselves, to the lands of their origin, to the countries in which they live. No survey of Christianity in Southeast Asia would be complete without considering their peculiar situations.

Fairly dependable statistics estimate that 1,360,000 Indians and nine million Chinese (aside from those in Formosa and Hong Kong) are scattered throughout Southeast Asia.

Chinese migration south and east goes back hundreds of years, and many Southeast Asian people have a strain of Chinese blood. There are separate colonies of Chinese throughout the area, however, and it is these groups that pose political, economic, and religious problems.

For centuries, these Chinese aliens felt tied to China only by family connections. It was the place to which they might return in their old age. The twentieth century brought a new rise of nationalism in China, however, and Chinese in foreign countries felt strong stirrings of patriotism. China today is a world power, and Chinese in Southeast Asia are conscious of it, even though most of them are carefully non-committal on political matters.

The estimate of nine million Chinese in Southeast Asia must be considered in comparison with a total population for the area of perhaps 180 million. These statistics aren't particularly accurate: census taking is a hard job in Southeast Asia, especially when different countries disagree in their definitions of who is Chinese.

The following statistics incorporate the results of surveys taken in 1947 and 1952:

	CHINESE POPULATION	CHINESE PROTESTANTS
Singapore	790,000	45,000
Federation of Malaya	2,000,000	(unknown)
Indonesia	2,000,000	60,000
Borneo	220,000	30,000
Philippines	150,000	3,500
Indochina	850,000	500
Burma	380,000	1,000
Thailand	2,500,000	2,000

The Chinese have formed their own communities wherever they have colonized. Separate schools, hospitals, churches, newspapers, and mutual benefit and protection associations make these communities resemble states within a state. The reaction of the people of Southeast Asia has been to protect themselves. Chinese residents have been subjected to restrictive laws; Chinese immigration has been reduced. The Philippines, for example, cut down the number permitted to enter and has deported some of the more undesirable ones. Thailand bars Chinese from voting or holding other than minor governmental positions. Indonesia is bringing pressure upon all aliens to eliminate dual nationality.

The Chinese exercise a high degree of control over the retail trade in every land of Southeast Asia. In Java, for instance, they are middle-men and money-lenders. They are the only middle class in most of the lands, a fact that conditions their church life as well as their position in the community. Their children go to separate schools; for thirty years the Chinese Government subsidized more than two thousand Chinese language schools abroad.

With the acknowledgement that this cohesiveness typifies the overseas Chinese, it is interesting to note that they have been more easily assimilated in predominantly Protestant areas of Indonesia (for example, Minahassa and Batakland) than in Islamic Java, the Roman Catholic Philippines, or Buddhist Thailand. There is evidence, too, that the alien Chinese is more open to the Christian gospel than has been the Chinese who did not leave China.

The majority of the Chinese who have moved southward came from southern China. Most widely dispersed are the Cantonese, who are found in Singapore and the Federation of Malaya, Indonesia, and the Philippines. Chinese in Southeast Asia speak their own dialects as well as the language of the countries where they live. English, the most widely used commercial tongue, is studied in most of the Chinese schools as the second language; in some it is the medium of instruction.

The desire of local groups of Chinese to retain contact with their homeland is expressed in the formation of Chinese chambers of commerce, clubs, and secret societies in almost every town. They are places where Chinese can feel at home abroad. It is no accident that though the Y.M.C.A. in China accepted large sums from the United States, and the Philippine Y.M.C.A. buildings were rebuilt after World War II almost entirely with American funds, the Chinese Y.M.C.A. in Manila refused foreign aid. Its building program was financed entirely with money raised locally; the second floor is occupied by the Chinese Chamber of Commerce, the top floor by a Chinese club.

Despite its resistance to change, however, the traditional social life of the overseas Chinese is showing signs of disintegrating under the impact of the West. Chinese intellectuals born overseas usually are closely connected with Western influences. They tend to eschew all religion, or if they become Christians, prefer Western churches. Thus Chinese congregations are composed of middle-class merchants and artisans, with only a smattering of teachers and other intellectuals. This condition explains the scarcity of ministerial candidates, the dependence of churches on lay workers, the susceptibility of the average congregation to the oratory of traveling evangelists.

The religions of China have not followed the Chinese southward. Communities of Chinese have in some instances erected Chinese temples, but the liturgy and services are vague and unidentifiable. The Ministry of Religions in Minahassa classifies all Chinese who are not Christians under the heading "Confucian-Taoist-Buddhist." The ties of the individual Chinese with his ancestral religions exists only in the family relationships and in clubs and societies.

While in isolated instances there was early Protestant work among Chinese in Southeast Asia, this was usually started by missionaries waiting for an opportunity to enter China. The concerted efforts now being made began late, sometimes only after national churches had been organized.

The beginning of missionary work among the Chinese in Indonesia was not the result of planning. Missionaries to the Church of West Java, frustrated by the unreceptiveness of the Islamic Sundanese, turned their attention to the more responsive Chinese. As early as 1858, a Chinese Christian community was organized at Indramaju. A Chinese church was organized by Dutch missions in Djakarta toward the end of the nineteenth century.

In the years preceding the opening of China to missionary endeavor, mission boards made elaborate preparations to seize the opportunity to enter when it came. Little effort was made to reach Chinese immigrants. Following the treaties of 1842, missionaries moved from Singapore, Bangkok, Batavia (Djakarta), and Borneo to Hong Kong and China's five open ports. They left little if any help for the Chinese population and congregations they had started. So despite early beginnings, there were but a few hundred Chinese Protestants in all Southeast Asia at the close of the nineteenth century.

Not until after World War I was significant work begun among the overseas Chinese. In Burma, the Methodists have taken the initiative; in Thailand, the Presbyterians; in Malaya, the Methodists, English Presbyterians, and Anglicans; in Indochina, the Christian and Missionary Alliance; and in Indonesia, Dutch and American missions. In the Philippines, the work among Chinese was started somewhat later by the United Church of Christ.

The position of the overseas Chinese has never been enviable. He has enjoyed more material prosperity than his hosts, due either to his energy and creativeness or the privileges accorded him by colonial powers. But he has been required to live in segregated quarters without the amenities of life available to Westerners. His future is clouded by the possibility of persecution or discriminatory legislation. Many of his traditional ties with his homeland have been cut, yet he has not sunk new roots in his adopted land. The uncertainties and the lack of security, combined with the power achieved by China under communism, have caused him to be sympathetic to, if not actually to embrace, the ideology of the new China. For those Chinese who feel the need for a dynamic philosophy of life, the choice at the moment is between communism and Christianity.

THE CHURCH IN HONG KONG

Hong Kong, chief jewel in the British crown and listening post for Communist China, was never so important for Christians as it is today.

It should be realized that Communist China's purposes are served by recognizing British sovereignty over Hong Kong. Western goods needed for China can be purchased and imported from the colony. There is a trickle of traffic across the border between Canton and Kowloon. Nationalist and Red spies touch elbows in the crowded streets. Thousands of Chinese refugees, including many Christians, have found homes of sorts either on Hong Kong Island or the leased territory adjoining it.

Even in the pre-Communist era on the Chinese mainland, Protestants engaged in some activities in Hong Kong. For example, an Anglican bishop was first consecrated in 1849.

The Church Mission Society operates a number of schools and hospitals in the Hong Kong-Kowloon area. The Methodist Missionary Society (of Great Britain), whose major center of work was in Canton, now concentrates its efforts in Hong Kong, where there are several strong congregations and schools.

Lutherans also had a minor early work in Hong Kong and the neighboring districts. This included an institute for Buddhists at Tao Feng Shan, which is now the site of a Lutheran Theological Seminary. In recent years, they have increased the number of churches and social institutions, ministering to more of the refugees and providing more facilities for the total colony.

American Methodists, Presbyterians, Baptists, the United Church of Canada, and others have followed a similar course, enlarging their staffs so that today more than seventy-five missionaries are engaged in evangelistic, relief, educational, and medical (leprosy) work. Two Christian colleges are developing to help meet the needs of the thousands of refugees who desire to continue their university studies. The United Board for Christian Higher Education in Asia and the Asia Christian Colleges Association (British) are giving aid to one of these institutions, and Yale-in-China is aiding the other.

The presence of a large number of missionaries and many well-educated Christian Chinese refugees has made possible a highly interesting church enterprise. This is the production and distribution of Christian literature for the millions of Chinese outside the Communist-held mainland.

In earlier years, the various religious publishing agencies in Shanghai had a federation whose purpose was to direct the distribution of Christian books and pamphlets. Most of the leaders of this agency fled from Communist rule and settled in Hong Kong. Organizing the Council on Christian

Literature for Overseas Chinese was a logical step. The council has a highly capable staff of Chinese and missionaries and a board of directors representing all Protestant groups in Hong Kong. It has reprinted some of the best literature formerly produced and distributed from Shanghai. In addition, a considerable number of new books have been published for the World Council of Churches and for Nanking Theological Seminary for distribution outside the China mainland. Centers for the sale of this literature have been established in most of the larger centers of Chinese populations in East and Southeast Asia.

Church World Service has given supplies and funds to refugees through various Christian organizations in Hong Kong. Typical of its assistance was the building of 180 houses for the victims of the Homantim fire in Hong Kong in January, 1953, which made thousands of squatters homeless. The Saviour Lutheran Mission added twelve more houses, so that approximately a thousand homeless persons were cared for. In addition to the dwellings, a community building was erected and is used as a nursery during the day and as a neighborhood center in the evening. The entire settlement has been given a Chinese name that means Faith-Hope Village.

Wesley Village, a similar home for refugees, has been established by Methodists from the mainland, aided by sizable grants from the American Methodist Committee for Overseas Relief, Canadian and British Methodist mission boards, and the United Church of Canada. Here, likewise, there is to be a social center and church.

Another of the major contributions being made by missions and churches to the life of the colony are schools.

Of the 340 schools being subsidized by the government, twenty are operated by missions. The buildings vary from one-room schools in the slums to finely equipped modern structures in other areas. All are crowded with boys and girls intent upon learning. There are few kindergartens. One of the best institutions is the Ying Wah Girls' School founded in 1900 by the London Missionary Society. The students include girls from both poor and well-to-do families. Few of the schools have playing fields adequate for sports and games because the area is so mountainous.

Christians also conduct many orphanages. One of these is at Fan Ling, under the auspices of the Hong Kong Evangelical Fraternity. One hundred and thirty-one abandoned children would be homeless but for this care. The Tai Po Orphanage run by the Church Missionary Society trains orphans to be farmers.

THE CHURCH IN TAIWAN (FORMOSA)

During the past century, mainland China absorbed a large proportion of the Protestant missionary effort. At one time more than eight thousand Western workers were engaged in evangelistic, educational, and medical activities. The net result of this activity was the development of a Protestant community of approximately a million persons. Roman Catholicism, dating back several centuries, claimed 3,266,000 Chinese.

Little is known about the life and work of the church on the mainland of Communist China. The government Bureau of Religious and Cultural Affairs supervises all the churches, which inevitably have become strongly patriotic. They assist in land reform, hold thought reform classes, and make their buildings available for political meetings. Church attendance is generally good in the cities, with a minimum of political propaganda in the sermons. The government claims that there is religious freedom and no persecution for religion. Christians have been imprisoned, but according to the officials the offenses were political. Home services of worship are on the increase. A decrease of church income has created grave financial problems, though the government makes grants for some Christian operations.

A seminary at Nanking has more than one hundred students; the president is Dr. K. H. Ting, one-time secretary of the World's Student Christian Federation. Said the Presbyterian Board of Foreign Missions in its report in 1953:

The Chinese people are undergoing a resurrection after the sleep of centuries. Whether this renaissance is to be for the final weal or woe of the Chinese people and the world is still hid from our eyes. In view of the suppression of liberties within the land, and the aggressive designs of the government outside of the land, the present trend is not reassuring.

Taiwan, the only part of China that is non-Communist, has been Chinese only since the end of the seventeenth century, when the Dutch were thrown out. Chinese migrated to the island in large numbers at this time and much of their way of life was eventually adopted by the people of Taiwan. A sizable portion of the tribespeople resisted the Chinese, however. These groups were predominantly Malay, related to the Igorots in the mountains of the Philippines. They were head-hunters and practiced ancestor worship.

After her victory in the Sino-Japanese War, Japan was given Taiwan in 1895. But up to the end of World War II, the Japanese had been unable to assimilate the tribes of the mountains. An electrically charged wire fence was maintained around their ranging area to keep them separated from the remainder of the population. Missionaries were forbidden to evangelize them, but the growth of the Christian church among these tribespeople was one of the major developments of the war and postwar period.

Protestantism in Taiwan falls into three distinctive periods. First was the Dutch. Three years after the Netherlands' forces landed in 1624, George Candidius arrived. He and the thirty-five Dutch Reformed workers who later served there until expelled in 1661 did much to redeem the excesses of a Dutch colonial policy. Five missionaries suffered martyrdom when the Chinese drove the Europeans from the island.

Few evidences of Christianity survived the two centuries that passed before Protestants again landed on the island. In the latter half of the nineteenth century, two missionaries reopened Christian work on Taiwan. They were Canadian Presbyterian G. L. Mackay and English Presbyterian Dr. James Maxwell, whose medical approach helped break down the suspicions of the people. Education later became an important element in the mission and church programs.

There followed a period of international wars, crises precipitated by attacks upon China by the great powers, and the ceding of Taiwan to Japan in 1895. Christians were suspect in each of these crises, and many suffered martyrdom. Veteran missionary Hugh MacMillan states that the basis of self-support, self-government, and self-propagation among the churches was formed during these testing periods.

Under the Japanese rule (1895-1945) education became an instrument of Japanese control, and Japanese became the language of instruction. By 1936, Canadian Presbyterian schools in the North had been taken over by the government, and Japanese directors had replaced the missionaries as directors in the English Presbyterian schools in the South. Two theological training schools had been combined into one at Taihoku. By the summer of 1941, all missionaries had departed. Schools and hospitals continued to operate. The churches survived in no small measure through unprecedented giving by Taiwanese Christians. The Christian organization was unified along the lines followed in Japan, a pattern dissolved only after the Japanese surrender. In 1945, the Presbyterian Church in Formosa was formed.

The third phase of Protestantism on Taiwan resulted from the Communist victory on the mainland, which drove thousands of Protestants to Taiwan. New congregations have been created out of the new arrivals. Sectarian groups have carried their distinctive approaches to former residents and newcomers alike, preaching to both non-Christian and Christian. The Joint Council of English and Canadian Presbyterians has expressed doubt as to the value of having so many new denominations. More than thirty missionary agencies have established work in Taiwan. Unfortunately, few of the leaders consulted the Presbyterian Church, the long-established church with major activities all over the island, before coming. The newly arrived missionaries work as separate units, the only cooperative effort being a summer conference of missionaries where most of the denominations are represented. Among some of the missionaries and Chinese Christians, there is a desire for greater cooperation, even for the establishment of a Christian Council. The religious climate is too divisive for quick results.

At Taichung, a large city on the West Coast, a Christian union university is being established, Tunghai by name. Its major buildings were dedicated in 1955, and the first class of students was received, selected from several thousand candidates who took the examinations. The United Board for Christian Higher Education in Asia sponsors this school and supports it in large part.

Alumni of Soochow University on the mainland operate an institution of higher education in Taipei, almost entirely on local support, but with small grants from the United Board and the American Methodist Board of Missions.

Quite successful evangelistic campaigns have been conducted by individual denominations or by groups of two or three working together. Much of this work has been carried forward among the two millions of Mandarin-speaking refugees from the mainland, but some of the missionaries now in Taiwan are also working among the Amoy-speaking Taiwanese.

Hugh MacMillan, writing the history of the church in Taiwan, has pointed out that the greatest gains were made during times of stress, when Christians were required to cooperate. In closing his account, he says of the Taiwanese church:

It is a young church, comparatively small in membership, inadequately staffed, lacking in material resources and surrounded by almost overwhelming tasks of evangelism in a society that is nearly 99 per cent non-Christian. Yet this church is conscious of its own missionary obligation to the unevangelized mass of the island's population, of the need of deepening and strengthening its own spiritual life and of sharing more in the rich heritage and experience of the older churches. It is beginning to be conscious of belonging to the world Christian community where each must aid the others in fulfilling the great commission to which Christ has called his people.[1]

INDIANS IN THE SOUTH SEAS

The Indians, like the Chinese, have been wanderers. Before the beginning of the Christian era, they had established colonies from Burma and Malaya to Indochina and what is now Indonesia. These outposts were cultural as well as commercial centers. The civilizations that developed in Thailand, Indochina, and Java, as evidenced by the remains at Auyudia, Angkor Vat, and Borobudor, were Indian in inspiration. In more recent times, as the British extended their colonial holdings in the nineteenth century, Indians moved to Burma and Malaya to become laborers and merchants.

The overseas population of Indians in Southeast Asia is centered mainly in Burma and Malaya today. About 600,000 live in Singapore and the Federation of Malaya. Burma is the home of 700,000. Sixty thousand more are scattered through the other countries of the area.

The Indians form compact communities that resist change. The customs of India and its villages are carried with them. They live as foreigners even though they become the majority race. Their clothing, their food, their customs are Sikh, Hindu, or Muslim, as the case may be, and the tensions between these groups are introduced. The Indians demand exemption from local rules and customs if they interfere with their own.

The tendency of the Indians to form religious communi-

[1] *Then Till Now in Formosa*, p. 96. Published by English and Canadian Presbyterian Missions in Formosa, 1953.

ties even in migration has meant that little Christian work has been done for or with them. Communities of Indian Christians in Singapore, the Federation of Malaya, and Rangoon have their own churches. They make limited attempts to reach non-Christians; additions to church membership by adult baptism are small.

Fiji provides an example. Ninety-nine per cent of all native Fijians are Christians, but only about one out of every seventy Indians on the island is a Christian. The Indian Christians have been won from a community that has little social contact with the Fijians, and make up a church that, though Methodist in name, is in fact a separate denomination from the Fijian.

The Fijians, who have taken the initiative in sending missionaries to several parts of the Pacific, are baffled by the task of making the Christian witness to the Hindu. This is due not only to the intransigence of the Indian community, but also to the Indian's belief that he is superior to the Fijian. Conflicts over property, legal restrictions on Indians, and the growing Indian population make the work of the church difficult. Slow progress is being made toward better relations. Some of the Christian schools enroll both Indians and Fijians, and in the doctrine of baptism and training of church membership, statements were adopted not for Fijians alone, but for the church as a whole.

The spearhead of the Methodist work among the Indians on Fiji has been a system of schools and dispensaries. At present, the church operates two secondary schools for Indians, the government one. As the government moves farther into this area, the church will be driven even more to make its distinctive purpose clear, a task rendered difficult by the secular nature of the Indian community. This is seen in the refusal of Indians and Europeans to observe Sunday, which to the Fijian is one of the marks of Christian behavior.

A. W. Loy, trained originally in India and now director of the Indian work in the Lautoka (western) district, writes:

Integration with the Fijian church has an importance which cannot be exaggerated. In any country the church ultimately finds that, of all the issues before it, there is essentially one which is the special task given it by God to fulfill for that time. In England a century and a half ago, it was the abolition of slavery; today in South Africa, it is the race issue; in India, it is the reunion of the church. If in these years we Methodists in Fiji maintain our comfortable, friendly separation, when the time of challenge and crisis comes we shall fail our Lord, and if we do so in a crucial issue in the life of this island, the Methodist Church will have become an irrelevant encumbrance on Fijian soil.

CHAPTER 15

The Unfinished Task

The Christian church in almost every land of Asia is a tiny David confronting an enormous Goliath of non-Christian religions and cultures, of communism and increasing secularism. The immensity of the task is a formidable challenge not alone to these young churches but to all of Christendom, East and West.

In this life and death drama, the mission still has a vital role to play. That role is to undergird the younger churches that now have the responsibility but lack the resources in personnel and money with which to do the job.

Unfortunately, the present Protestant approach to the non-Christian world overseas is essentially the same as it was in the early days of missions. Each denominational or confessional agency goes where it wills. In pioneering days, such a method was not a serious handicap; there were so many unworked fields that any group might choose for itself the place of primary interest. No longer is this true. There is a surfeit of workers in some regions, scarcity in others.

In contrast, the Roman Catholic Church has a global program. For example, the Vatican admittedly has set out to win the Batak people in Sumatra. In the region where Dutch or American Roman Catholic missionaries are unacceptable, they are replaced by priests or lay workers from nations for which the Indonesians have friendlier feelings. Areas on the island that are predominantly Protestant are flooded with Catholic schools in an effort to win the young.

NEED FOR NEW PROTESTANT APPROACHES

World Protestantism is slow to accept the leadership and planning that the International Missionary Council could provide by way of a united, comprehensive approach to missions. Until such an over-all program is followed, the Protestant groups will continue to misdirect and dissipate their resources. Unless global, interdenominational planning is adopted, the Protestant churches probably will continue to send people and money to areas that have sentimental appeal or that are important economically or politically for their homelands. And, because the younger churches, like the older ones, are partly conditioned by nationalism, they will accept a similar pattern for themselves.

During and after World War II, some Western church agencies devised the Orphaned Missions approach. Regardless of their own denominational or racial background, they contributed to a central fund administered by the International Missionary Council. The money was used to help missions in Asia and Africa cut off from the churches supporting them. Orphaned Missions functioned regardless of nationality, creed, or denomination. There are many Christian leaders, especially among the overseas churches, who believe such strategy is a pattern for things to come.

Not alone in deployment of missionaries, but in their selection and training, the Christians in the West must change their policies.

The limitations under which Protestant missions operate today in Southeast Asia are so stringent that only well-qualified, well-trained, properly adjusted persons should be commissioned as missionaries. Governments are increasingly demanding that Western personnel possess technical skills valuable to the life of the nation where they serve. Be they doctors, teachers, theologians, social or audio-visual workers, they should be good in their speciality and adaptable to changing conditions. They must be patient, too, while the churches of Southeast Asia learn how to use their talents.

More Americans of Negro, Oriental, Indian, and Mexican ancestry should be appointed as fraternal workers and missionaries. The Student Volunteer Movement and the missionary education branches of the churches should aim their appeals toward junior and senior high school youth in these groups, and must help them obtain scholarships and study aids in order to prepare specifically for overseas work.

Deputations of Christian students, professors, and other lay people should be sent to Asian lands for periods ranging from several months to a year so they can have firsthand contact with the younger churches and their institutions. Congregations in the West should give their ministers leaves of absence to be spent on mission work. Care in screening would be necessary in order that the right persons be placed in the right places. Equal attention should be given to preparing them for overseas experience.

Missions, in most denominations, are extra added attractions for local churches. Consequently, mission agencies are almost tragically limited in resources and personnel. The younger churches suffer, in turn, because they cannot get the help they need from overseas. There is insistent need to generate a new drive and passion for missions in the older churches.

One of the powerful forces during the rapid expansion of America's missionary interest flowed from concern for individual souls. Dr. Robert E. Speer, speaking at an early Student Volunteer Movement conference, asked for a period of silence of one minute. At the end, he profoundly impressed the audience by announcing that many thousands of persons had died during that time without having heard the gospel of eternal salvation.

Western Christians today need to feel again the urgency of evangelism. It is still true that thousands die daily without Christ. What is still more tragic is that millions live without Christ. The evangelization of the world in this generation and every generation is the continuing responsibility of the total world Christian community. Until the acceptance of this responsibility generates a burning passion to proclaim everywhere the good news, we will in effect be denying Christ no less effectively than did Peter during the early morning trial of his Master.

Another driving force in the early missionary movement was an inspired determination to save the world by spreading social justice and peace. This was not, and is not, a substitute for evangelism, but it is an essential part of the Christian approach to a needy world. The Good Samaritan was a central figure in Jesus' teaching, and the modern Good Samaritan remains one of the major forces in God's process of redemption.

MISSION RESPONSIBILITIES: EAST AND WEST

World War II changed the relationships between Christians of East and West. Some of the mission boards and missionaries have found it difficult to adjust to a new environment in Southeast Asia. Experiments must be conducted with patience on both sides. The Western churches have to discover how to work in today's situations. The Southeast Asian churches in turn must become aware of the worth of the resources that come from the Western Christians and learn how to conserve and use those resources.

The churches of Asia want to help one another. They must be assisted in doing so. They have only limited financial resources. They cannot, and probably should not, organize mission boards on the American pattern. But they are experimenting. Already, the Methodist Church of the Philippines has sent a missionary to Okinawa, and the Church of Christ in the Philippines has sent three missionaries to Thailand and a missionary couple to Indonesia. Two Indian missionaries are attached to the Batak Church in Sumatra, their salaries covered by the Lutheran World Federation. Malayan Methodists support a Chinese from their own number and two Batak Christians from Sumatra in missionary work in Borneo among the Dyaks.

In 1954-55, two lengthy consultations of missions and churches from widely separated parts of Asia were held in Hong Kong, looking toward forming an agency to clear requests for interracial and international missionaries and to seek financial support for such workers. For more than a half century, the Wesleyan Church of Fiji has sent workers to adjacent islands, to New Guinea, and to the aborigines of Australia. The Methodist Church in Australia assists in this project, and other churches of the West might do something similar to enable educated men and women of Asian lands to serve as fraternal workers on the staffs of other churches in Southeast Asia.

Missionary promotion and education in the sending lands have been centered upon missionary personnel and their individual accomplishments. It has seldom created an awareness of the overseas church that has come into being, of the function of that church as a dynamic witness to Christ as Lord and Saviour, or of the individual members and leaders of the church who are the living witnesses.

Likewise, a large proportion of the missionary dollar is expended on the support of missionaries and the hospitals, schools, and social institutions they have helped to found. Only a small fraction is available for the active extension of the gospel through Southeast Asia's churches and their leaders. This kind of distribution is out of date today in most situations. With the autonomous churches beginning to claim exclusive responsibility for the total Christian operation within their areas, the churches of the West must help devise a new formula. The formula should provide the needed resources whereby Southeast Asia's churches can take the total responsibility in their own lands for "missions in the new age."

This new idea of the place of the overseas church in the outreach of Christianity must become a center of attention of Americans. It is relatively easy to raise support for a missionary whom church members can see and hear. It is much more difficult to find help for the churches that have developed from missionary service. Yet it must be done.

The unfinished task of bringing Christianity to Southeast Asia lays heavy responsibility on Western churches. But from the viewpoint of Southeast Asia's churches, the job is even more formidable and demanding.

PROBLEMS OF THE YOUNG CHURCHES

In the first place, *they are minority churches*. Only in the Philippine Islands is Christianity a majority religion. The people are predominantly Roman Catholic; Evangelical churches include but 3 per cent of the total population. The proportion is slightly higher in Indonesia. In Malaya, Indochina, and Thailand, Protestants are fewer than one per cent of the total population, and in Burma approximately 2 per cent.

Protestant converts are primarily won from tribal peoples who live in the hills or more primitive areas. Only in the Philippines and Indonesia are Protestants a cross-section of the nation. In Burma, Thailand, and Indochina, most of the Protestants live in rural areas and country towns. In Malaya, Indonesia, and the Philippines, they are found in both urban and rural areas. Christian communities on the whole are economically poor, struggling to eke out a livelihood from the land, usually employing crude methods of agriculture. They have not outthought nor outlived the non-Christian religions. The iron curtain of Islam, the impenetrability of Buddhism, the confusion of races and languages, the clash of modern ideologies and resurgent cultures, the antagonisms of nationalism—these are problems that stubbornly defy quick or easy solutions. The Christian communities must study modern developments in the non-Christian religious systems. The churches must approach educated non-Christians with intelligence to meet their special needs. Literature must be produced to clarify the Christian position.

They are alien churches. They represent the outreach of Western Christianity. Foreign missionaries brought with them the life, thought, and polity of their own churches. The resultant similarity between the Asian and the Western churches has caused the former to be dubbed "ecclesiastical colonies." They have imported their architecture, music, theology, and church polity wholesale from the West. Their foreignness to Asia has repelled rather than attracted men to Christ.

Islam and Buddhism, on the other hand, have flourished in many parts of Southeast Asia. The secret of their success lies in the fact that they penetrated the cultures of the countries to such an extent that the faiths shed their foreignness and became domesticated. They were not like alien potted plants; they took root in the soil of each of the lands they entered.

In contrast, Christian churches have not been left free to grow in Eastern soil without interference from the planters. Dangers from compromise, syncretism, and heresy admittedly exist, but such dangers must be faced to allow free growth. Yet the churches must be rooted in Christ before they can be related to the soil. They must safeguard the purity of the Christian faith by reliving the experiences of redemption, being crucified and risen with Christ. They must make clear to themselves and to others the unique Lordship of Christ. "Foreign" they must be, for their citizenship is in heaven. But they also must live and spread in the soil and climate of individual lands. Under the guidance of God, they must transform local ideas and traditions, rejecting everything unworthy and conserving all they have learned in Christ, so that the eternal gospel may be expressed in the temporal language and life of the people.

They have few leaders. The level of leadership in the Southeast Asian churches varies from country to country. Those churches that regard Christian schools as essential have produced educated leadership. But in Thailand, Malaya, Indochina, and Indonesia there was not even a single Christian college prior to 1953, when a Christian university was founded in Djakarta. Judson College in Rangoon was closed after World War II, leaving only the Philippines with Christian colleges of standing and tradition. Education may not be the main task of the church, but it is the one way of reaching the educated and ruling classes and of training church leaders.

An educated Christian community in a non-Christian land extends the Christian influence over the entire nation. Educated Christians in the Philippines, Burma, and Indonesia have an influence out of proportion to their numerical strength. A church without trained leadership cannot assume the responsibilities that a foreign mission, which is in process of relinquishing its authority, would like to transfer to it.

A living and growing church must have an educated ministry. This need is largely unfulfilled in most lands of Southeast Asia. Churches in Burma, Thailand, the Federation of Malaya, and Singapore recruit few candidates for the ministry. The churches in Indonesia, Burma, and the Philippines have only partially satisfactory facilities for the training of adequate Christian leadership. Nine tenths of the ministerial functions in Indonesia are performed by unordained, part-time preachers who earn some or all of their income as teachers, farmers, etc. Malaya is experimenting with a similar type of ministry.

They must achieve self-support. This support involves adequate pay for ministers, provision for evangelism, and assistance to neighboring weaker churches. The Karen Church in Burma, the Batak Church in Sumatra, and the Church of Viet Nam have attained this status, not because of any economic prosperity of their members, but because of their emphasis upon tithing and stewardship. Their giving has a spiritual basis.

The majority of the churches in Southeast Asia are dependent upon Western financial resources. An Asian church dependent upon foreign funds will be regarded by non-Christians as a foreign church, a tool of ecclesiastical imperialism, suspect, and the object of contempt. Self-governing Asia demands that the churches also maintain their self-respect by paying their own way.

This does not mean that all foreign support must be terminated immediately. Christians help the weak and the poor. Churches cannot accept the narrow-minded nationalism that, because of national pride, refuses outside help when it is needed. Christian life teaches the grace both of giving and receiving.

SUMMING UP

One hundred and eighty million people live today in Southeast Asia. Protestant church membership is less than four million, or fewer than one in every forty persons. Vast areas with as many as 10 million inhabitants have no church or place of Christian witness. Relatively few converts have been made from Islam and Buddhism. Numerous ethnic and racial groups have still to be reached with the Christian message. Ancient religions have taken a new lease on life, and these resurgent faiths deny the exclusive claims of Christianity. Militant communism preaches that religion is the opiate of the people and purposes to destroy it to establish a system based on materialism. Secularism and atheism are gaining ground.

The church of Christ in Southeast Asia is living and working against such odds. It lacks resources of men and money. The church beckons to its partners to come to its aid and, in obedience to Christ, undertakes with them the extension of his kingdom in the East. Two and a half per cent, with God, is a significant minority.

The new chapter in missionary history fills one with hope. The Asian churches are becoming mission minded. They, too, are sending their sons and daughters as missionaries of the Cross. Indonesia and Malaya have long been mission fields of the Chinese churches, and the church in Malaya has now begun to send its own missionaries. Churches in the Philippines have sent missionaries to Thailand, Indonesia, and Okinawa.

A medical fraternal worker and a theological teacher among the Bataks in Sumatra come from the Tamil (India) Lutheran Church. A Cambodian Christian is preaching to his fellows in Thailand, where Karen Christians from Burma are also at work. They are but symbols of the Southeast Asian awakening to the fullest meaning of the Great Commission.

While the evangelization of Southeast Asia may be undertaken in partnership between the younger and the older churches in obedience to His will, the primary responsibility of winning Southeast Asia to Christ rests upon the churches whose stories are told in this book. Djakarta, Bangkok, Manila, Singapore, Saigon, and Rangoon are suburbs of the City of Man in Southeast Asia. The gospel reminds us that they are meant to be suburbs of the City of God.

READING LIST

LEADERS of adult study groups are directed to *Adult Guide on "Southeast Asia,"* by Doris Dennison, published by Friendship Press at 50 cents, and to the other Friendship Press books listed below for a complete program of materials to supplement *The Church in Southeast Asia.* All publications of Friendship Press are available through denominational book stores and literature depositories.

Views expressed in the books of other publishers, listed here for further resource reading, are not necessarily in harmony with those of the authors and publishers of *The Church in Southeast Asia.*

FRIENDSHIP PRESS BOOKS

East from Burma, by Constance Hallock. Cloth $2.50, paper $1.25.

Living Religions Series:
   Introducing Buddhism, by Kenneth Scott Latourette.
   Introducing Hinduism, by Malcolm Pitt.
   Introducing Islam, by J. Christy Wilson. Each 60 cents.

Christianity and the Asian Revolution, edited by Rajah B. Manikam. $2.50.

Pattern of Things to Come, edited by Dorothy McConnell. Cloth $1.50, paper 75 cents.

Revolution and Redemption, by M. M. Thomas and Paul E. Converse. 60 cents.

Mission Unlimited, by S. Franklin Mack. Cloth $2.00, paper $1.25.

Give and Take, by Herman C. Ahrens (fiction based on fact). Cloth $2.50, paper $1.25.

Ann of Ava, by Ethel Daniels Hubbard. Cloth $2.75, paper $1.50.

Dauntless Women, by Winifred Mathews. Cloth $2.75, paper $1.50.

Eagle Books (stories of missionaries in Southeast Asia):
  #1. *If Only I Had a Ship*, by Basil Mathews.
  #5. *My Friends the Cannibals*, by Cecil Northcott.
  #26. *The Book in the Pillow*, by Pat Yates.
  #38. *Send Me Among Savages*, by Cecil Northcott. Each 25 cents.

BOOKS OF OTHER PUBLISHERS

A History of South-East Asia, by D. G. E. Hall. New York, St. Martin's Press, Inc., 1956. $10.00.

Asia East by South, a cultural geography, by Joseph E. Spencer. New York, John Wiley & Sons, Inc., 1954. $8.50.

Christianity in the Philippines, by Dwight E. Stevenson. Lexington, College of the Bible, 1955. 50 cents.

Crusade in Asia, by Carlos P. Romulo. New York, The John Day Co., 1955. $4.00.

Economic Change in Thailand Since 1850, by J. C. Ingram. Stanford, Calif., Stanford University Press, 1955. $5.00.

Hungry Billions, food, health, and education for the underdeveloped areas, by Donald K. Faris. New York, Harper & Brothers, 1956. $5.00 (price subject to change).

Indonesia: Land of Challenge, by Margueritte Harmon Bro. New York, Harper & Brothers, 1954. $4.00.

Japan's Role in Southeast Asian Nationalist Movements, by Willard H. Elsbree. Cambridge, Harvard University Press, 1953. $3.25.

Jungle Green, by Arthur Campbell. Boston, Little, Brown & Co., 1954. $4.00.

Leprosy Missions in Southeast Asia, a pamphlet, by Gene Phillips. New York, American Leprosy Missions, 1956. Free.

Malaya: Communist or Free?, by Victor Purcell. Stanford, Calif., Stanford University Press, 1954. $3.00.

Men Against the Jungle, by Richie Calder. New York, The Macmillan Co., 1954. $3.50.

Minority Problems in Southeast Asia, by Virginia Thompson and Richard Adloff. Stanford, Calif., Stanford University Press, 1955. $4.00.

New Nations of Southeast Asia, by William Henderson. New York, Foreign Policy Association, 1955. 35 cents.

North from Malaya, by William O. Douglas. Garden City, N. Y., Doubleday & Co., Inc., 1953. $3.95.

Report from Malaya, by Vernon Bartlett. New York, Criterion Books, 1955, $2.75.

Representative Government in Southeast Asia, by Rupert Emerson. Cambridge, Harvard University Press, 1955. $3.50.

South-East Asia: A Short History, by Brian Harrison. New York, St. Martin's Press, Inc., 1954. $3.50.

South-East Asia Between Two Worlds, by Tibor Mende. Toronto, Smithers & Bonellie, 1955. $4.50.

Southeast Asia in the Coming World, edited by Philip W. Thayer. Baltimore, The Johns Hopkins Press, 1954. $4.75.

The Roots of French Imperialism in Eastern Asia, by John F. Cady. Ithaca, N. Y., Cornell University Press, 1954. $5.00.

The Struggle for Indochina, by E. J. Hammer. Stanford, Calif., Stanford University Press, 1954. $4.00.

A WORD ABOUT THE FORMAT

The text of this book was set on the Linotype in 10 point
Janson, leaded 3 points. This fine old face was designed by
Anton Janson some time between 1660 and 1687. The Linotype recutting was made direct from the original matrices and
retains the sharpness and sparkle of the original.

Composition, press, and binding: QUINN & BODEN
COMPANY, INC., Rahway, New Jersey · Jackets and
paper covers: AFFILIATED LITHOGRAPHERS, INC., New
York · Map: modeled by RAFAEL PALACIOS and re-
produced from Kodachrome negative by AFFILIATED
LITHOGRAPHERS, INC. · Text paper: S. D. WARREN'S
#66 ANTIQUE.

TYPOGRAPHICAL DESIGN BY MARGERY W. SMITH
BINDING BY LOUISE E. JEFFERSON